HOW TO MAKE
Working Decoys

HOW TO MAKE

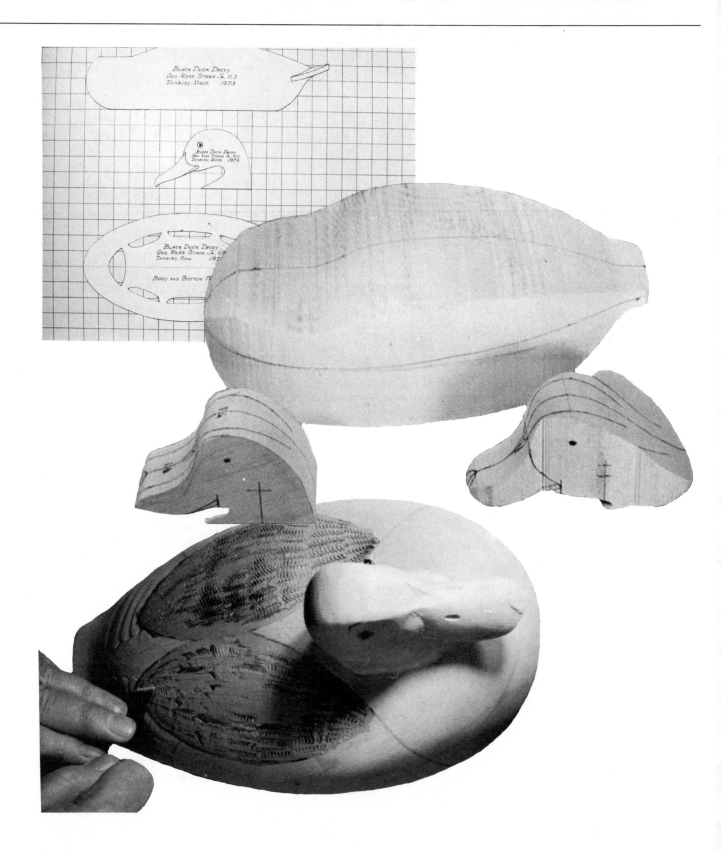

Working Decoys

George Ross Starr, Jr., M. D.

Photography by ANDREA PAPE

Winchester Press

An Imprint of NEW CENTURY PUBLISHERS, INC.

THIS BOOK
is dedicated in humble admiration to
that very rare and special breed of duck hunters
and carvers who developed the working decoy into
the marvelously efficient working tool it has become—
and those now and in the future who
will make them even better.

Printing code
14 15 16 17
Library of Congress Catalog Card Number: 82-62595

ISBN 0-8329-2609-4
Printed in the United States

Contents

Introduction

W̲HEN YOU COME RIGHT DOWN to it, there is obviously a philosophy of wildfowl decoys. Man has been around for a long time, and birds have been around even longer. It was inevitable that, as a phase of man's continual search for food, they would cross paths with each other. Unlike all the other living things that man has hunted, birds could escape quickly into the air, thus presenting an entirely new set of problems to the hunter. Trapping was somewhat successful but involved a lot of permanent equipment and, except in the settled areas of Western Europe, has never been widely used. The Indians of our own Southwest have been credited with making the final deduction that the best way to be most sure of getting birds would be to entice them within the range of the bow and arrow. Tethered live birds would obviously do a fine job, but it was reasoned that easy-to-handle replicas would work nearly as well and so the wildfowl decoy was born. Although these Indian decoys represented very fine workmanship (FIGURE 1), much remained to be done toward refining the art of making decoys. The canvas-back illustrated was one of a dozen found in the excavation of Lovelock Cave in Nevada. They have been dated by the carbon method at more than one thousand years old. These decoys are on exhibition at the Museum of the American Indian in New York City and are well worth a trip to see.

The first step in developing a decoy philosophy is to establish a definition of a working decoy that will encompass all the factors that affect its making and use. There is, of course, one perfect decoy for every species—a live bird of the same species. Unfortunately for the modern hunter, the use of this wonderful ploy was outlawed about fifty years ago, and it is extremely doubtful that the law will ever be repealed. Before a lot of tears are shed over this situation, remember that a live decoy presented some problems as well as great advantages. It had arrived at that plateau that so many labor unions are now trying to obtain: the "guaranteed annual wage." No matter how much or how little it worked during the gunning season it had to be given bed and board for the entire year. It is for this reason that during the market-hunting years many professional gunners simply could not afford to keep a flock of live decoys. The margin of profit was just too small. This leaves us with just one answer—an artificial duck.

A working decoy, therefore, has to be a symbolic representation of a living bird. The key word is "symbolic," since no decoy can be a complete replica of a living bird. Unless it is sound asleep on an ice floe, the chief characteristic of a live bird is almost constant motion. There is really no way to impart the same kind of natural motion to a flock of wooden decoys. By the use of good body design, variations in position, keels, and weights, we can impart an almost natural or contented look to a decoy spread, but it is far short of the real thing. There are men who can create such an accurate reproduction of a bird that, if placed in a flock, you could have great difficulty in picking it out—until all the others get up and fly. On the other hand, a rig of birds of such caliber would be far too prone to injury and breakage to be much good under the average gunning conditions. And so we must accept that by definition a working decoy must be an example of the best symbolic carving and one that will present the correct plumage pattern, appear as natural as possible in the water, and still withstand the wear and tear to which it will be subjected in the course of a gunning season.

As gunning spread to the other areas of the country, and particularly after the white man arrived armed with smoothbore firearms, it was soon found that no one type of decoy would work well in all situations. The evolution and development of the decoy thus proceeded slowly and steadily over the years. It is certain that the original decoys used in the Barnegat Bay area were solid, but as the Barnegat Bay sneak box gradually assumed its final form, these decoys were found to be much too heavy. By making the decoys hollow, just as many could be carried with the additional advantage of easier handling and much greater safety because of the decreased weight in the boat while getting to and from the hunting site.

A different set of conditions determined a different decoy design as the battery method was developed in the shallow waters of the Susquehanna flats at the northern end of Chesapeake Bay. Here it was found that the birds would decoy best out in the open water and that the more decoys used the better—up to as many as six hundred in a rig. The battery itself was put in the water and anchored in place and then the "stool boat" circled around to set out the decoys. Because of the great numbers involved, the decoys were simply tossed out on the water with anchor lines freed. There was no time to go around and straighten decoys that had landed upside down or on their sides, so a heavily weighted decoy with a semivee bottom was designed that guarantees that no matter how it is thrown it will always right itself immediately. The weight of an individual decoy was of no particular matter here since the stool boat was so large.

Duck shooting along the Maine coast gave decoy makers an entirely different set of problems—rough offshore waters and heavy tides and currents. It was soon discovered that a larger-than-life-size decoy is more visible in rough water than is the normal size. On the other hand the exposed positions made fewer decoys work as well as a great number since there was nothing else around to distract any birds who showed interest in the rig where the open water gave a greater sense of safety. It was also worked out that by using a flat bottom, a really wide beam, and a relatively low body height, most decoys did not need weights on their bottoms. Maine is about the only area where weights were not widely used.

Down along the Connecticut shore, at the mouth of the Housatonic River in the town of Stratford, a particularly fine type of hollow wooden decoy was developed that gave great performance under the local conditions. There are salt marshes and open water with the added complication of slushy ice due to the fresh water coming down the river. The decoys usually have a rather high bluff bow to ride over the slush rather than be dragged under by it.

It is all very well simply to say that this decoy comes from one region and that decoy from another, but this does not explain why we can pretty well guess their place of origin. The big part of the "why" is that by study and research we have come to understand the requirements of a decoy for any given area. I cannot believe that any of this was accidental. We have to assume that the first decoys made and used in an area were probably very crude and that when they did not function as well as it was thought they should, it was then that the more analytical and imaginative makers came forward with improvements. Knowingly or not, these men were working on the principle that form follows function and as the function of decoys became better understood, the modifications in form necessarily followed. Not every man who was capable of making some sort of decoy was capable of making any overall improvement. But when one man did create a marked improvement in style and design and subsequently proved it in action, it was only a short time before others began to copy it. With each such change the final style for each area gradually became established.

This book will not be restricted to a set of patterns and a band saw, but is directed much more toward stimulating the potential decoy maker to create his own designs and patterns to give him the most effective decoy for the area in which he hunts. The various areas will be covered to give due credit, when known, to the men who brought about the final form and to analyze their contributions. The basics of decoy design will be presented and all practical materials will be evaluated. The various tools which can be used in decoy production will be described and the techniques of using them will be illustrated. Numerous photographs will show each stage of layout, body carving, head carving, assembly, and painting.

The question quite naturally arises as to why anyone in his right mind would even think of making a decoy in the first place when there are so many good commercially made ones on the market. Well, I think there is a very good answer to that question. Many years ago Goethe said: "To do something, you must be something." If you really enjoy beautiful and satisfying things, if you have a deep urge to use (or try to use) your hands in creative effort, if you truly love all the aspects of duck hunting in fair weather and foul, if you truly enjoy observing wildfowl in flight and on the water, and if you never before thought of making a decoy, then make one and "be something." And—from one who will never stop trying—the best of luck!

—George Ross Starr Jr., M.D.

Duxbury, Massachusetts, 1978

HOW TO MAKE
Working Decoys

CHAPTER 1

Design

OVER THE LAST CENTURY many decoys have been made commercially and have had wide distribution nationally—those from the Mason Decoy Factory, formerly located in Detroit, Michigan, are the outstanding example. Except in certain specific cases, the same models were sold country-wide with no allowance made for any variations in local gunning conditions. Thousands were sold and on the whole they worked well.

However, in about 1850, the age of the market gunners began and they soon became the greatest users of decoys. In general they avoided the use of commercial decoys for two very compelling reasons. In the first place, despite what we would consider·ridiculously low prices compared to now, they simply could not afford them. Secondly, and even more important, they gradually developed designs and styles that would produce the best results in any given area. From this came the wide varieties of decoys which are now so eagerly sought by collectors.

The man who wants to make his own working decoys must first make a set of decisions that will go a long way toward determining what form those decoys will eventually take. Not all species are found in all hunting areas, so you must first determine which birds are available in your own area and which of these in the greatest numbers. When you have this information, you will know which species of decoys will give you the greatest return for the effort you are going to put into making them.

Once the species have been selected, an analysis of the actual hunting conditions of your area must be made to reveal the most practical and successful sizes and styles of decoys. Because my experience has been chiefly along the East Coast, the first factor I consider is the amount of wind that can be expected on the days when shooting should be at its best and, in particular, what effect it will have on the decoys. Heavy wind over open water creates chop, which tends to make decoys bounce around much more than is natural. As a matter of fact, 8 to 10 knots of wind actually produces whitecaps. Therefore, decoys used this way have to be much bigger and wider than normal in order to overcome as much as possible the tendency to bob around—remembering all the time that the bigger they are the more work they are to handle. If you plan to shoot at the edge of open water in the lee of a point or a wooded area where much calmer water can be expected, great oversize decoys are not needed. The principle of finding the one spot of calm water when the wind is howling everywhere else is the true essence of setting out decoys for maximum results. Water depth is also an important factor in relation to wind— the greater the depth of the water the more wave action any given velocity of wind will produce; so the shallower the water you can gun over, the less you have to worry about the effect of wind on decoys.

Another factor to consider, which happily occurs only along open water and coastal marshes, is the matter of tide. Those who are not subject to it can be very thankful. North of Cape Cod the tide runs from 8 to 13 feet—and much more as you go farther east. What is a sparkling sheet of water at noon will be a vast mud flat cut by a few small channels at six o'clock. A marsh river, which is 150 feet wide when you set up at its edge at high tide, dwindles to a channel 20 feet wide and 10 feet below you six hours later. Tides like this force two rules on you when using decoys: don't figure to handle more than a dozen and be sure the lines are long and the weights heavy.

Once the tide problem is handled, you still must set out and pick up the decoys. First consideration must be given to the actual size of the decoys used. Advertising seems to pay in the decoy business as well as in any other—oversize decoys seem to work much better than normal or undersized ones. This can be carried to extremes in certain cases. The old goose stands along the New England coast had, of necessity, to compete with each other for the flocks of geese making their way south. In addition to the live beach and flyer teams, normal-size decoys were placed just off the blind. To top all this, display groups of increasingly larger decoys were anchored at an eighth and a quarter of a mile off the blind. The quarter-mile geese were great slatted affairs, often as much as 5 feet in length. Fortunately, these monsters were left out for the entire season. Oversize decoys are fine if you are in a spot where they work better and if they don't add to your labors of setting out and picking up.

The next concern must be the weight of each decoy. If you are in a situation with a permanent blind on the shore and relatively shallow water in front of it, no matter what their weight, decoys can be set with a minimum of effort. If on the other hand you must set out and pick up from a boat, the task becomes that much more onerous. Few chores in this world are worse than picking up a big and heavy—and probably iced up—decoy from a boat in midwinter. The early market gunners evolved a method of alleviating some of this discomfort by making the large decoys of a lighter construction. The usual method, which is not used any more except for swan decoys in North Carolina, was to construct a frame of wood or wire that was covered with slats or canvas. This method was pretty much restricted to coastal and offshore areas and generally was used only for scoters ("coot" in New England), eiders, and geese, where visibility from a great distance was a distinct advantage.

The size and weight of each decoy must be balanced against a third factor for each hunting area—the most advantageous number of decoys to use. When Russ Burr and his friend shot the streams and small ponds in New Hampshire, they used only six relatively small black ducks and it worked out fine. Since some places required a mile hike through the woods, lugging a regular rig of full-sized decoys would have ruined the whole expedition. George Scott, who introduced me to duck hunting in 1949, still uses only seven oversize black duck decoys for his successful hunting in Duxbury Marsh. Battery shooting for canvasback and redheads on the Susquehanna Flats at the head of Chesapeake Bay was another matter entirely. This was no one-man effort but a team operation. Not only did the battery itself have to be taken out and anchored in the correct position, but as many as six hundred decoys were set out around it—and picked up when the day was done.

When contemplating making a working decoy rig, the local gunners in your area can give you the best advice as to size, numbers, and the makeup of the rig. Although the prime duck of your area is the mallard, should you set some teal out with them early in the season, or should you make some pintails to add to the set for later shooting? A few bluebills along with the blacks may help to slow down a few passing divers, but in Narragansett Bay a bluebill rig should run from eighty to a hundred and twenty decoys for guaranteed results. I don't believe that any one hunter knows all the answers to all the areas, but with a little effort you can find a man who knows what you will really need for where you want to hunt. Find him and take his advice before you buy wood and start hacking away at decoys.

The basic question facing the decoy maker is whether to make his decoys solid or hollow. The answer to that will determine the dimensions of the lumber you must order or cut locally. The earliest wooden decoys were solid and this is still the rule in many, if not most, places. A solid decoy requires only two parts—a body and head—with no more work involved in assembly than fastening the head to the body. Before choosing hollow decoys, be certain that the lessened weight and somewhat higher flotation will produce enough additional birds to make the increased work worthwhile.

Rather than present many decoy plans in this book, I want to stimulate the prospective maker to be responsible for every phase of the decoy he makes—from the designing and planning through the construction steps to completion. I know his pride will be that much greater if it is all his own work. The very best advice that

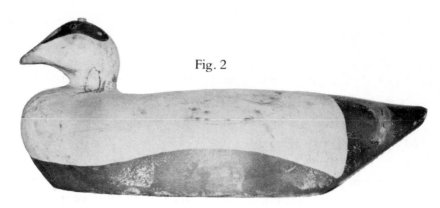

Fig. 2

Fig. 4

FIGURES 2, 3, 4. Eider drake made about 1900 by Captain Pinkham of Seguin Island lighthouse, Maine. 23¾ × 9 × 23¼ × 10 × 5¼″

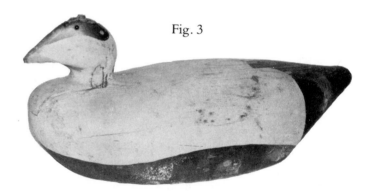

Fig. 3

can be given from the design angle is to study old decoys and incorporate their finest features in your plans; however, this advice isn't much help to someone who doesn't know what features to look for. To remedy that situation I have selected a couple of decoys from each of the main hunting areas and will point out the characteristics by which they illustrate the distinguishing design quirks of their makers—which make them so outstanding as successful decoys. Each decoy has been photographed from three different angles along with a 2¾-inch twelve-gauge shell. In order to save the work of calculating actual dimensions from the shell length, a series of five numbers will be found in each caption which will show: (1) length from bill to tail, (2) head height, (3) body length, (4) body width, and (5) body height.

The eider drake in FIGURES 2, 3, and 4 shows the propensity of the old Maine carvers to make decoys larger than life to increase their visibility. This rig was made

18

about 1900 by Captain Pinkham of Seguin Island lighthouse from a spar that was washed ashore after a big storm. The wide, thick body made for easy riding in a heavy sea and good visibility for incoming birds. No bottom weights were ever used on this decoy—a credit to its stability. Another fine Maine example is the whitewing scoter in FIGURES 5, 6, and 7. The actual maker is unknown, but he is definitely from the Monhegan Island–Penobscot Bay area. The primaries are in low relief, a characteristic of this area. Both birds show the inlet head so common in Maine. It really doesn't make sense to go to all the extra work of cutting the head block into the body when it does nothing to strengthen the neck itself. Why and how this style developed is something I have never been able to find out.

Two men in Massachusetts spent their lives as hunters and designers and builders

Fig. 5

Fig. 6

Fig. 7

FIGURES 5, 6, 7. Whitewing scoter from the Monhegan Island-Penobscot Bay area, by an unknown maker. 18⅝ × 8 × 18¾ × 7⅞ × 3⅞″

19

Fig. 8

Fig. 9

FIGURES 8, 9. Canada goose made by Joe Lincoln of Accord, Mass.
25¾ × 12½ × 24 × 10 × 6¾"

of decoys and each developed a marvelously beautiful and workable style for this area. Joe Lincoln of Accord made the solid Canada goose in FIGURES 8 and 9. Note particularly the clean and simple lines that made it possible to produce these decoys with a minimum of labor. Joe always painted in the afternoon and left the decoys sitting out overnight because he believed that the morning dew would improve the colors and make the paint set better. These decoys really last, with a minimum of upkeep. Many of them are still in use locally, sixty and more years after they were made. Joe's friend Elmer Crowell, of East Harwich, turned out thousands of birds over the years. His earlier birds were quite crude, and he made several design changes before arriving at his final style about 1910, as seen in the redhead in FIGURES 10, 11, and 12. On his "top" grade birds, Crowell did a very simple carving of three primaries and took a couple of swift cuts on the tail to add a little class. Although the original paint has suffered quite a bit, he did yeoman service over the years.

Fig. 10

Fig. 11

Fig. 12

FIGURES 10, 11, 12. Redhead made by Elmer Crowell of East Harwich, Mass.
16¼ × 8 × 14 × 7½ × 4¼″

21

The Stratford area carvers on the Connecticut shore developed a style of decoy that since 1850 has worked particularly well under the conditions found locally—a big freshwater river flowing into a large salt marsh area. If you are faced with the same problem, Benjamin Holmes provided the answer in the black duck in FIGURES 13, 14, and 15 made in 1876. The high and narrow breast cuts through the slush ice which forms when salt and fresh water meet. Most Stratford birds were hollow but, as you can see, it was often not an equal-halves deal but a heavy body block hollowed from below and sealed by a ⅝-inch bottom board. The profile view shows a "tear drop" weight, which will be described in a later chapter. Quite a number of advanced decoy collectors believe that the finest working decoys from the Stratford area were made until very recently by a man named Lou Rathmell. His black duck (FIGURES 16, 17, and 18) is made from compressed cork and has almost perfect black duck lines. It would be a fine pattern for a novice to use the first time out. The tail, which is normally the most breakable part, is formed by a piece of wood set into the stern of the body. Lou did not fool around with bottom weights that might snag and so weaken the cork, but cut a piece of lead the correct size, positioned it, and then set it in flush with the bottom of the body.

For many years a lot of Long Island decoys were made with natural cork as the body substance. This practice supposedly started because many ships were lost off the south coast and the old life jackets would drift ashore eventually. The jackets were made from slabs of natural cork, averaging about 1¾ inches in thickness, rather than compressed cork. The brant in FIGURES 19, 20, and 21 is a typical example. The cork slabs were fastened together by cedar pins driven in at angles. Although they have the advantage of light weight, they represent a phase of decoy history no longer in use.

Fig. 13

Fig. 14

Fig. 15

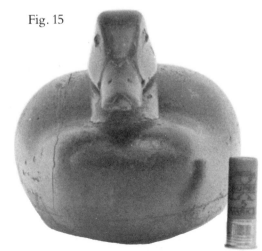

FIGURES 13, 14, 15. Black duck made in 1876 by Benjamin Holmes of Stratford, Conn. 16½ × 5⅝ × 15⅛ × 6½ × 4″

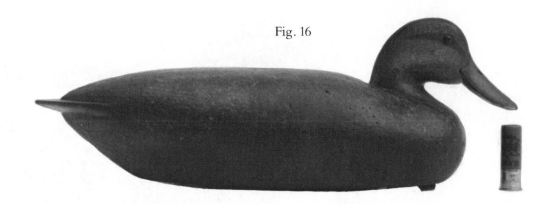

Fig. 16

Fig. 17

Fig. 18

FIGURES 16, 17, 18. Black duck made by Lou Rathmell of
Stratford, Conn. 17¾ × 5¾ × 15¾ × 6¾ × 3¾″

24

Fig. 19

Fig. 20

Fig. 21

FIGURES 19, 20, 21. Brant made of natural cork slabs, from Long Island. 16¾ × 9¾ × 14¼ × 7½ × 3½″

About 1955 Bill Joeckel made the solid bluebill drake in FIGURES 22, 23, and 24 for use in his working rig. It is an excellent decoy and merits great consideration from any neophyte who wants to make decoys. Notice the compact design and comfortable low head with nice wide jowls. There was a simple round weight on the bottom but no keel.

The Barnegat sneak boat was developed in New Jersey and is a most efficient hunting machine; however, its small size restricts the space that can be used for carrying decoys. This in turn led to the design of somewhat undersized, very light hollow decoys, known locally as "dugouts," quite large numbers of which can be

Fig. 22

FIGURES 22, 23, 24. Black duck made about 1955 by Bill Joeckel of Long Island. 13¼ × 5¼ × 12 × 6¾ × 3½"

Fig. 23

Fig. 24

26

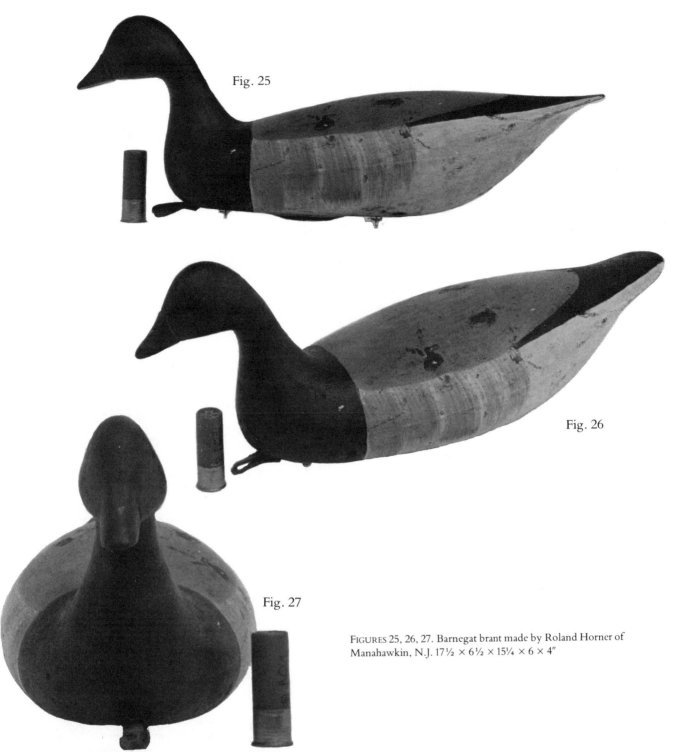

Fig. 25

Fig. 26

Fig. 27

FIGURES 25, 26, 27. Barnegat brant made by Roland Horner of Manahawkin, N.J. 17½ × 6½ × 15¼ × 6 × 4″

stowed on the deck of a sneak boat. One of the finest of the local makers was Roland Horner, who made the brant in FIGURES 25, 26, and 27. Note the fine sweeping lines and the two-piece construction. Bottom weights on Barnegat decoys are either set in flush with the bottom or sheets of lead whose edges are hammered to a bevel, so they can be nailed flat to the bottom with no ridges or sharp angles that might injure another decoy when they are stowed in the boat.

The most prolific of the Jersey makers was probably Harry Schourds, who made the black duck in FIGURES 28, 29, and 30. This old well-used bird clearly shows the seam line of the body halves with some of the old white lead caulking now visible. The simplicity of Schourds' plans and the elimination of all details enabled him to make these decoys in record time.

Over on the Delaware River a style was much used that was characterized by highly raised and joined primaries (FIGURES 31, 32, and 33). Just why this was done has never really been adequately explained to me. This black duck is an example to the beginning decoy maker of what not to do. These fancy primaries add a tremendous amount of work without basically increasing the effectiveness of the decoy in use.

Fig. 28

Fig. 29

Fig. 30

FIGURES 28, 29, 30. Black duck made by Harry Schourds of New Jersey. 15¾ × 6¾ × 14 × 6 × 4″

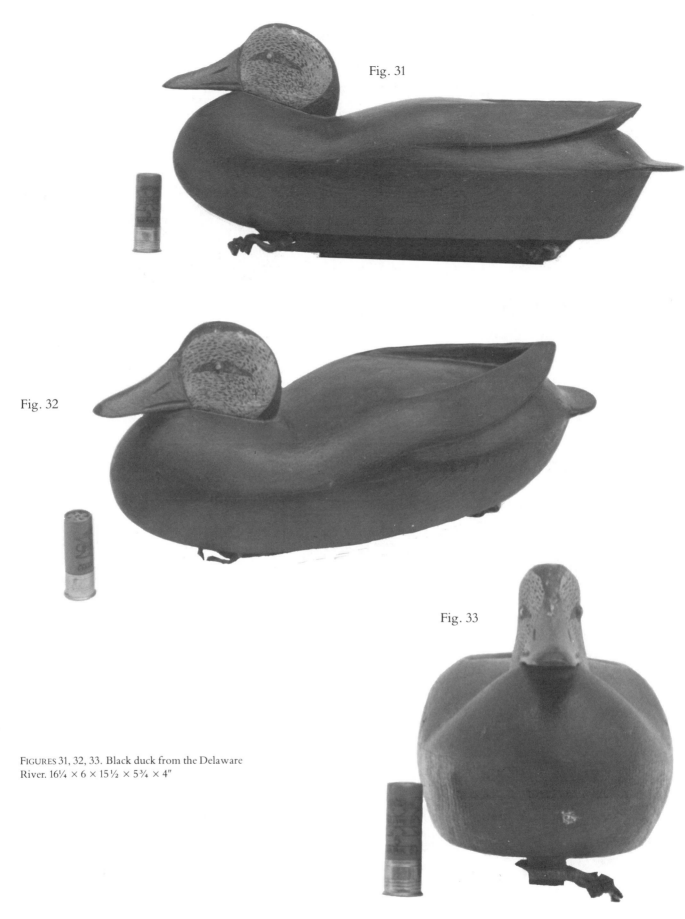

Fig. 31

Fig. 32

Fig. 33

FIGURES 31, 32, 33. Black duck from the Delaware River. $16\frac{1}{4} \times 6 \times 15\frac{1}{2} \times 5\frac{3}{4} \times 4''$

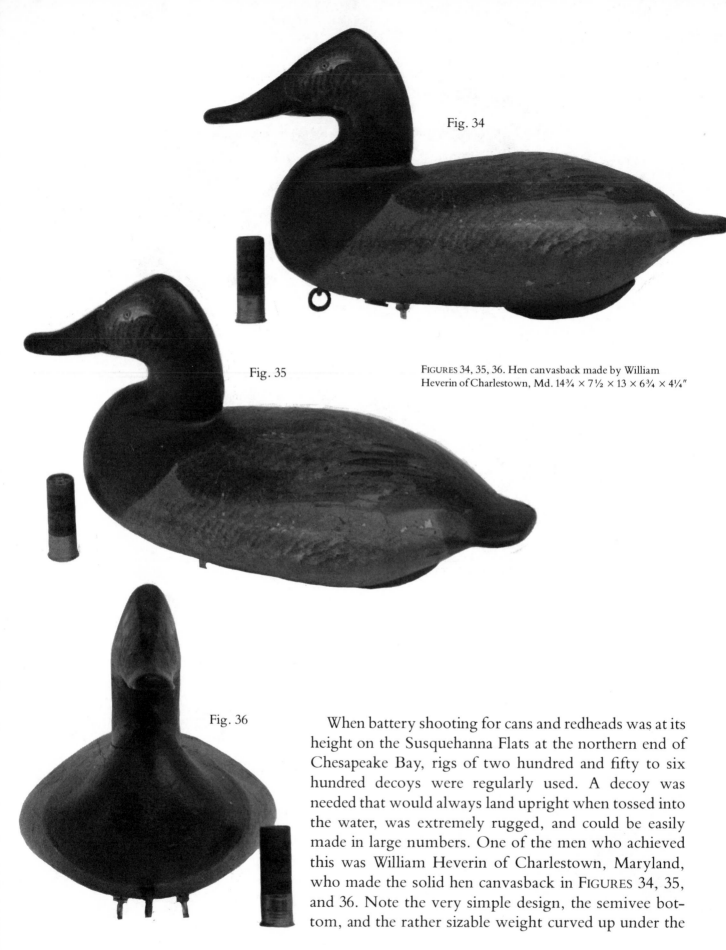

Fig. 34

Fig. 35

FIGURES 34, 35, 36. Hen canvasback made by William Heverin of Charlestown, Md. 14¾ × 7½ × 13 × 6¾ × 4¼″

Fig. 36

When battery shooting for cans and redheads was at its height on the Susquehanna Flats at the northern end of Chesapeake Bay, rigs of two hundred and fifty to six hundred decoys were regularly used. A decoy was needed that would always land upright when tossed into the water, was extremely rugged, and could be easily made in large numbers. One of the men who achieved this was William Heverin of Charlestown, Maryland, who made the solid hen canvasback in FIGURES 34, 35, and 36. Note the very simple design, the semivee bottom, and the rather sizable weight curved up under the

FIGURES 37, 38, 39. Pintail hen made about 1936 by Lem and Steve Ward of Crisfield, Md. 16½ × 6¾ × 14½ × 6½ × 3¾″

Fig. 37

Fig. 38

Fig. 39

tail to ensure it will always right itself no matter how it lands in the water. Lem and Steve Ward, down the Bay at Crisfield, made a large number of very fine decoys over many years. The new decoy maker might like to know that these brothers changed their style and design many times and made no bones about it. Most of us favor the style they used about 1936—an example of which is the pintail hen in FIGURES 37, 38, and 39. Don't let the simple construction of this bird take your eye away from its really lifelike qualities.

As one proceeds down the coast, even the most successful decoys show a lot less attention to detail than the ones farther north. The black duck in FIGURES 40, 41, and 42 was made by Ira Hudson, one of the old famous carvers of Chincoteague Island in Virginia. Note the rounded body and the presence of tool marks that were not sanded down. The paint pattern is very simple and the body feathers can be seen finely scratched into the final coat. From Poplar Branch, North Carolina, comes the massive canvasback made many years ago by Ellie Saunders, the grandfather of the present clan (FIGURES 43, 44, and 45). Note the semivee bottom for battery use and the boldly carved but unsanded body and head. The bottom weight is a crude iron casting, presumably of local origin. Maybe this isn't the style of decoy a new maker might like to use as a model, but under the conditions for which it was intended it worked.

One area with very distinctive decoy styles which until quite recently not only has been neglected but undeservedly looked down upon is Louisiana. Here in the bayou country one finds the most sheltered and quiet waters, and local material has been used to make decoys that are ideal for the conditions. Only the lowest 2 to 3 feet of the butt of the tupelo gum wood tree are used for decoys because from there on up the wood becomes much heavier and more dense. Tupelo is extremely light, carves easily, and stands up very well, given the favorable gunning conditions. Mitchell LaFrance, who is nearing the century mark and is probably the oldest carver in the nation, is still actively carving decoys. His pintail drake in FIGURES 46, 47, and 48 has all the characteristics of the best Louisiana decoys—small, light, and colorful. Note that the wings are in quite pronounced relief and the plumage pattern does not waste effort on subtleties.

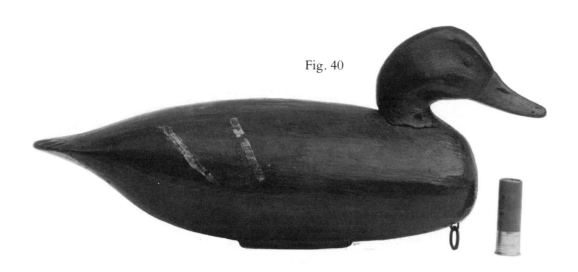

Fig. 40

Fig. 41

Fig. 42

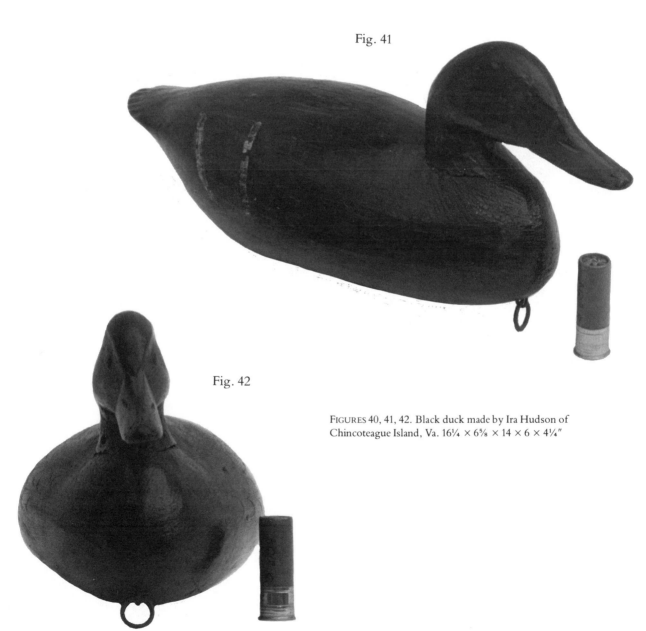

FIGURES 40, 41, 42. Black duck made by Ira Hudson of
Chincoteague Island, Va. 16¼ × 6⅝ × 14 × 6 × 4¼″

Fig. 43

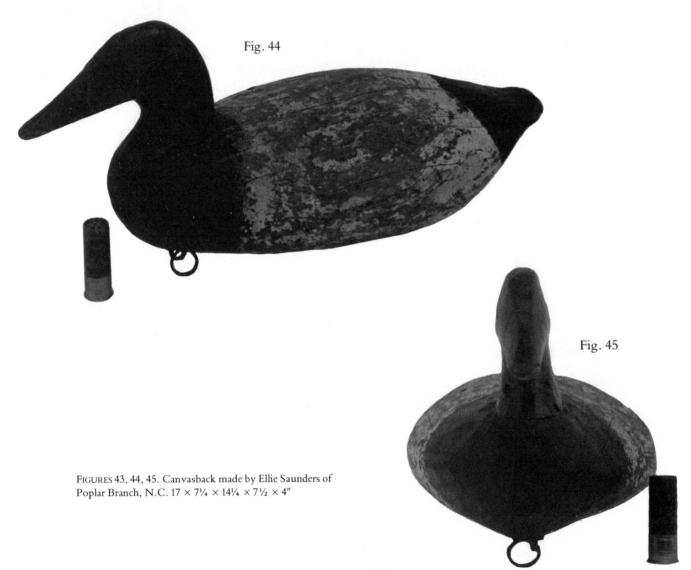

Fig. 44

Fig. 45

FIGURES 43, 44, 45. Canvasback made by Ellie Saunders of
Poplar Branch, N.C. 17 × 7¼ × 14¼ × 7½ × 4″

Fig. 46

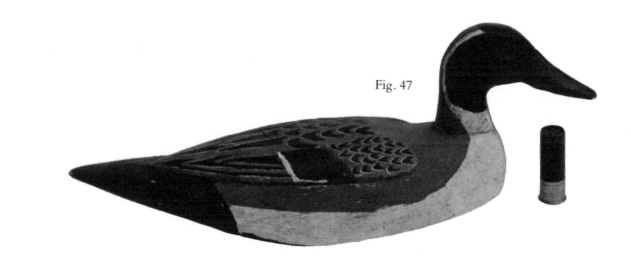

Fig. 47

Fig. 48

FIGURES 46, 47, 48. Pintail drake made by Mitchell LaFrance of Louisiana. 16⅛ × 5¾ × 13¼ × 7½ × 4″

35

A second maker with a flair all his own was Mark Whipple, whose ringbill is shown in FIGURES 49, 50, and 51. It is tiny and pert with a most simple but effective plumage pattern; and just to prove that bulk isn't always essential, it weighs just 9 ounces.

Coming back up north again, we come to the solid bluebill hen in FIGURES 52, 53, and 54 by Chauncey Wheeler of Alexandria Bay on the St. Lawrence River. Here again are simple lines that are easy to reproduce. This bluebill affords examination of a chine, which is the angle at which the sides meet the bottom on a boat. A "hard" chine implies a flat bottom and a 90 degree angle with the side. Wheeler used the hard chine to help the decoy ride more steadily with less roll. Across the river in the province of Ontario the decoy-making habits were somewhat different, although the gunning conditions didn't differ that radically. One of the outstanding makers was D. K. Mitchell of Brookville, whose bluebill hen is shown in FIGURES 55, 56, and 57. The Canadians went in heavily for feathering, most of which was done by specially made steel tools that are struck by a hammer to produce the indentations. (Similar tools used by Ben Schmidt are described later.) This little bird was hollowed from the bottom in an oval shape into which was fitted a thin butternut board that is finished flush with the bottom of the bird—a fine piece of work with much to offer the beginning designer.

Fig. 49

Fig. 50

Fig. 51

FIGURES 49, 50, 51. Ringbill made by Mark Whipple of Louisiana. $10 \times 6\frac{1}{8} \times 9\frac{1}{2} \times 4\frac{1}{8} \times 3\frac{1}{4}''$

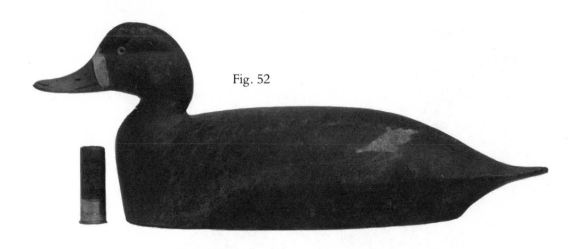

Fig. 52

Fig. 53

Fig. 54

FIGURES 52, 53, 54. Bluebill hen made by Chauncey Wheeler of Alexandria Bay on the St. Lawrence River. 16½ × 6¼ × 14 × 6 × 3½"

Fig. 55

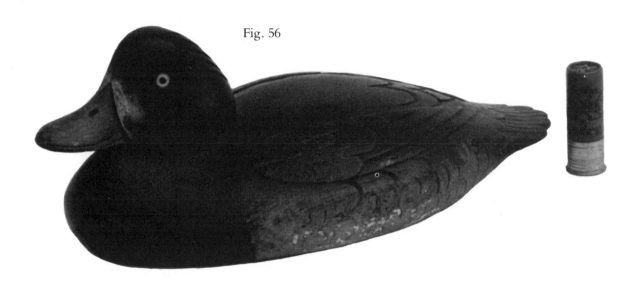

Fig. 56

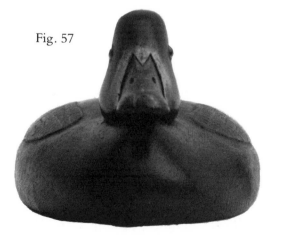

Fig. 57

FIGURES 55, 56, 57. Bluebill hen made by D. K. Mitchell of
Brookville, Ontario. 12 × 4½ × 11½ × 5¾ × 2½″

One of the most prolific of the Michigan makers was Ben Schmidt of Centerline, whose redhead drake is shown in FIGURES 58, 59, and 60. Ben made a real working decoy with a fairly hard chine and good wide beam. The primaries are cut in quite crudely with files and both the body and head have an unsmoothed file finish. The plumage pattern is effective but not detailed or elaborate. The head design is particularly good. Ben was never beyond experimenting. This bird was drilled out from the bottom, while an almost matching redhead hen in my collection is solid and has a keel with a long weight. In my own opinion this decoy would work well anywhere.

If you want to start out by jumping into really fine and imaginative decoy design, try something like the decoy in FIGURES 61, 62, and 63. It was made by Nate Quillan, who was a gunner and maker for one of the gunning clubs in the marshes along the St. Clair River in the Detroit area. The name of the game was lightness and contentment. You see him now as a bluebill drake, but he started life as a redhead drake. Someone decided to change his species and had the bad judgment to use an air brush and paint, which cannot be removed without damaging the original. The low resting head not only creates a quiet atmosphere but at the same time eliminates the neck, which is the weak point of any decoy. Quillan hollowed this bird from the bottom, leaving a very thin shell and then used only a ¼-inch bottom board so that it weighs only 14 ounces. It originally had a keel and, I assume, some sort of weight for added stability.

The towns along the Illinois River produced an amazing number of decoy carvers, thanks to the wonderful gunning in the area. They developed a moderate-size decoy that was hollow and usually had a rounded bottom—actually not too different from the Barnegat style. My own favorite was Charles Perdew of Henry, Illinois, whose mallard drake is shown in FIGURES 64, 65, and 66. For a bottom weight he used a cast lead strip with his name in relief.

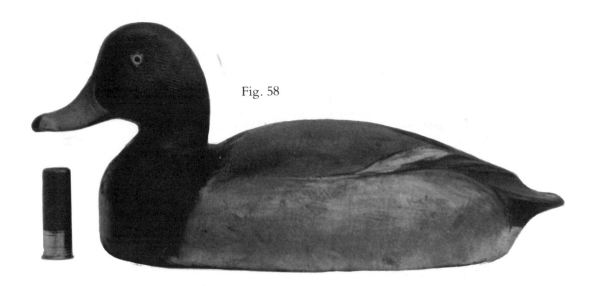

Fig. 58

Fig. 59

Fig. 60

FIGURES 58, 59, 60. Redhead drake made by Ben Schmidt of Centerline, Mich. 14½ × 6⅛ × 12¾ × 7⅜ × 3¾″

41

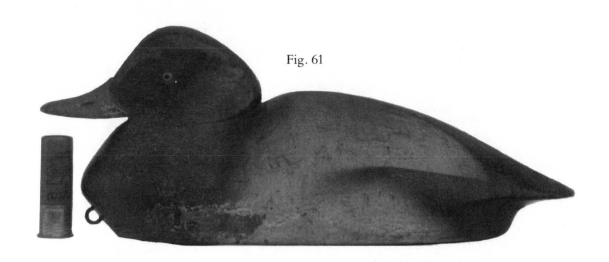

Fig. 61

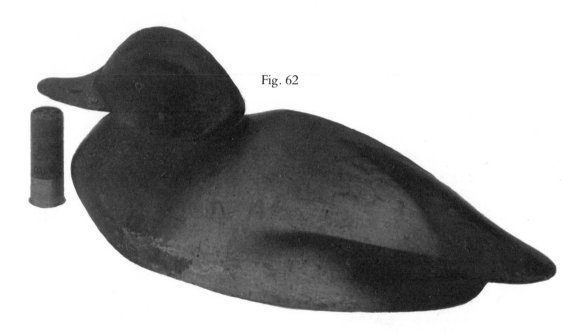

Fig. 62

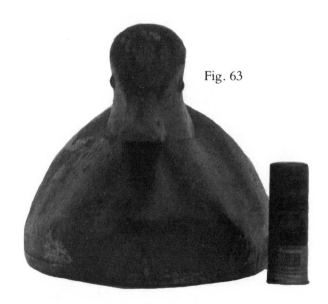

Fig. 63

FIGURES 61, 62, 63. Bluebill drake (originally a
redhead drake) made by Nate Quillan of the St. Clair
River area, Mich. 13 × 5 × 12 × 5¼ × 3⅜″

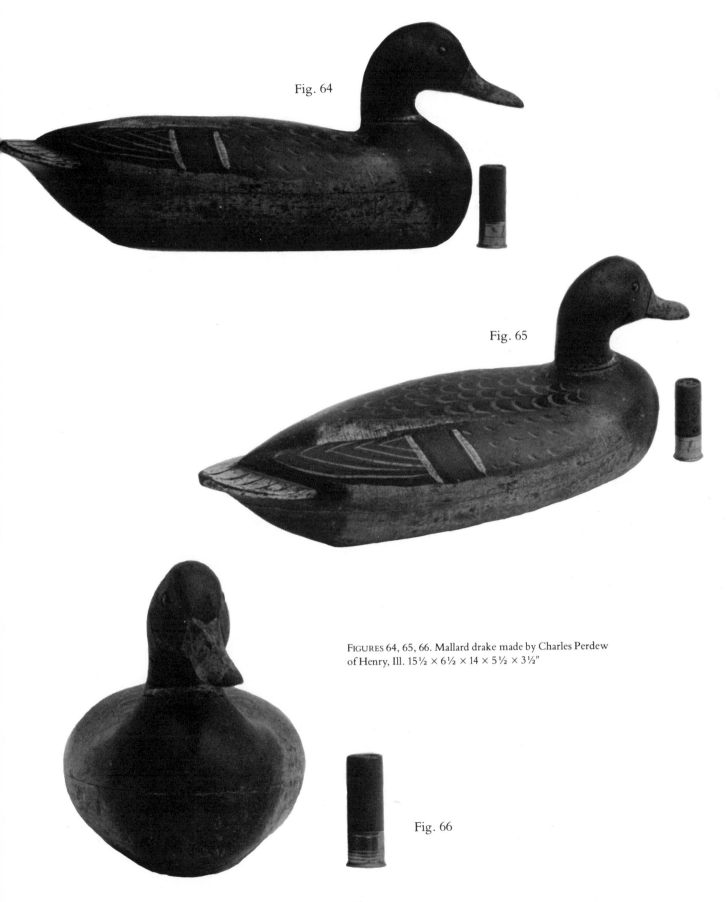

Fig. 64

Fig. 65

FIGURES 64, 65, 66. Mallard drake made by Charles Perdew of Henry, Ill. 15½ × 6½ × 14 × 5½ × 3½″

Fig. 66

Fig. 67

Fig. 68

Fig. 69

FIGURES 67, 68, 69. Pintail drake made by Amiel Garibaldi of the Pacific flyway, Calif. 16½ × 8⅝ × 14 × 4½ × 4″

Fig. 70

Fig. 71

Fig. 72

FIGURES 70, 71, 72. Pintail from the Pacific flyway, Calif.
6¼ × 4½″

Out in California on the Pacific flyway gunning revolves around rice fields and pintails. The solid drake in FIGURES 67, 68, and 69 was made by Amiel Garibaldi and is a very fine working decoy. The chief feature from the design angle is the high neck—true of pintails but in this case a little bit higher to make certain it is visible from afar. If you are looking for a design that saves on labor and lumber, try the "artichoke head" pintail decoy in FIGURES 70, 71, and 72. What body there is is hollowed from the bottom. The boys out there claim that the birds are so plentiful you don't even need a whole decoy to bring them in.

The best way to use this book is to pick a decoy pattern that requires all the techniques and follow it through from the plans to the completed decoy, painted and in the water. The work of Charles "Shang" Wheeler of Stratford, Connecticut—one of the truly great decoy makers—would be an excellent place to start. In 1948, Shang Wheeler and Joel Barber collaborated on plans for a hollow scaup—broadbill—bluebill decoy that uses most of the techniques of decoy making. Charlie Disbrow, also of Stratford, was a great and close friend of Shang's and after Shang died many of his decoy materials went to him. Included in the patterns were the plans for the bluebill in FIGURE 73. These plans are photographed on a 1-inch grid, and are the ones that are used in this book.

You will notice that at the lower right are two patterns for a sleeping head for this bird that were not part of the original set, because they were added by me. It is easy to draw a sleeping head over the original patterns, but I am not artistic enough to be sure what it will look like when rendered in wood. Therefore, I have gotten into the habit of making a rough half-scale model in Plasticine to make sure I have the proportions right. In FIGURE 74 is a half-scale pattern of the top profile and bottom plan fixed with rubber cement to a ½-inch grid. Plasticine is piled on the pattern (FIGURE 75) and the sides cut to the size of the pattern (FIGURE 76). A small ruler is

FIGURE 73. Plans for a bluebill made in 1948 by Charles "Shang" Wheeler and Joel Barber of Stratford, Conn. The plans, photographed on a 1-inch grid, are shown in Figures 74–92.

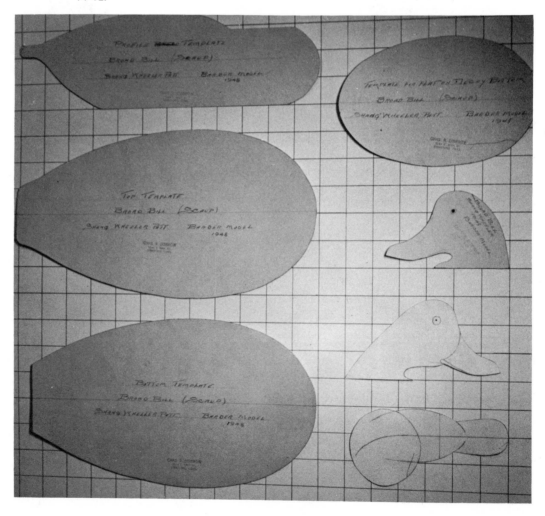

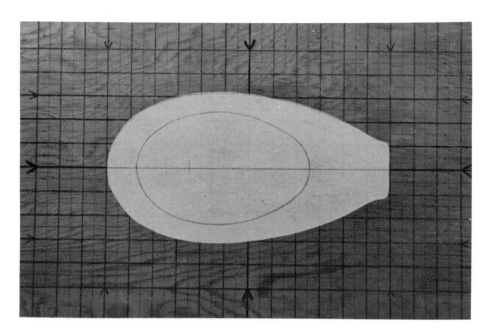

FIGURE 74. Half-scale pattern of the top profile of Wheeler and Barber's bluebill, fixed to a ½-inch grid with rubber cement.

FIGURE 75. Plasticine is piled on the pattern of the bluebill.

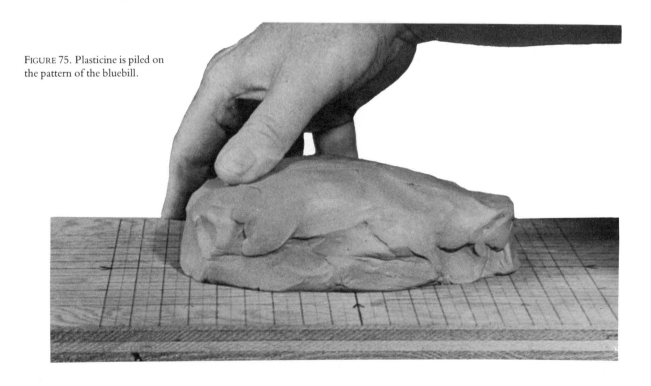

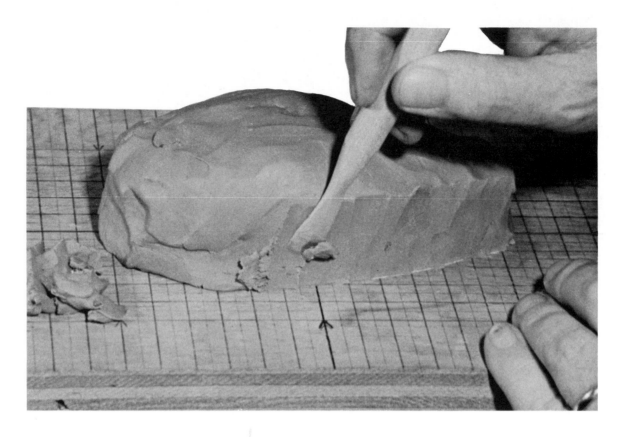

FIGURE 76. The sides are cut to the size of the pattern.

held against a square to make a cut for the correct body thickness (FIGURE 77). FIGURE 78 shows measuring the tail height and beginning to undercut. A line is drawn around the body to mark the line of maximum beam (FIGURE 79). We proceed to further undercut the tail and start curving under from the sides to meet the bottom pattern lines in FIGURE 80. FIGURE 81 shows more undercutting and the shaping of the aft end of the body toward the tail. In FIGURE 82 the back end of the head seat is marked, and in FIGURE 83 the height of the head seat is marked. Cutting the flat area for the head seat (FIGURE 84) and measuring how far back the tip of the bill will be (FIGURE 85) are the next steps. In FIGURE 86 Plasticine is piled on for the head and in FIGURE 87 excess head material is cut away. FIGURE 88 shows the rough shaping of the head by hand and FIGURE 89, the undercutting of the head. FIGURE 90 shows the final smoothing of the bird with fingertips, and FIGURES 91 and 92 display the final form with the pattern lines of the head inscribed.

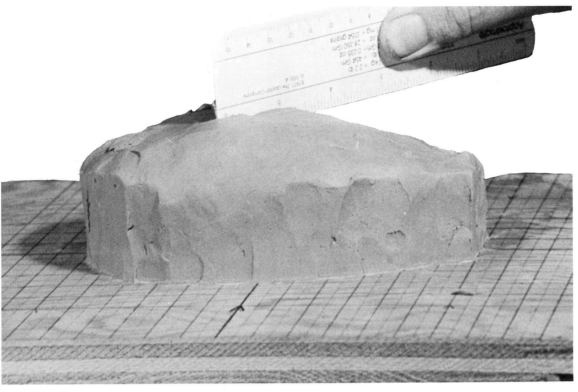

FIGURE 77. A small ruler is held against a square to make a cut for the correct body thickness.

FIGURE 78. Measuring the tail height and beginning to undercut.

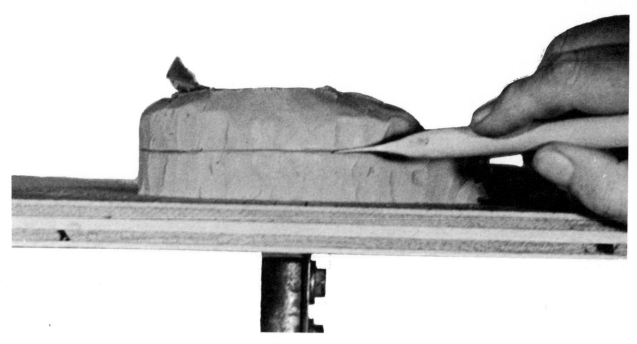

FIGURE 79. A line is drawn around the body to mark the line of maximum beam.

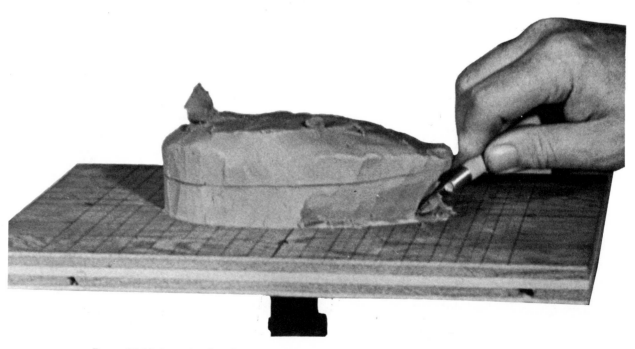

FIGURE 80. Undercutting the tail and curving under from the sides to meet the bottom pattern lines.

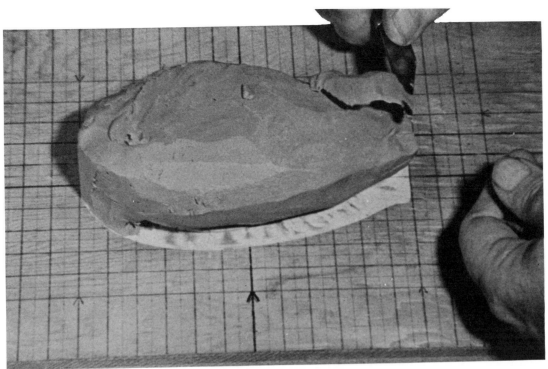

FIGURE 81. Shaping the aft end of the body toward the tail.

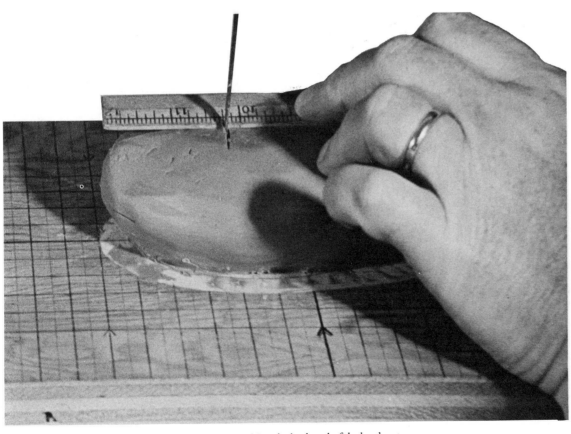

FIGURE 82. Marking the back end of the head seat.

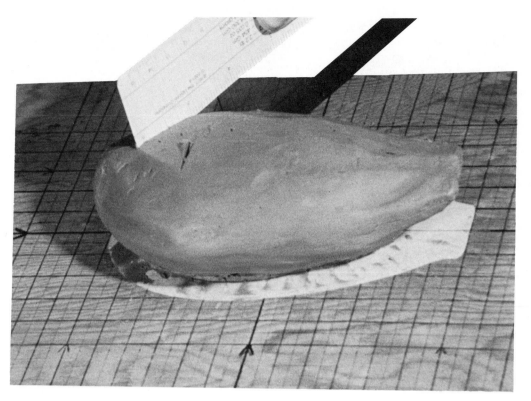

FIGURE 83. Marking the height of the head seat.

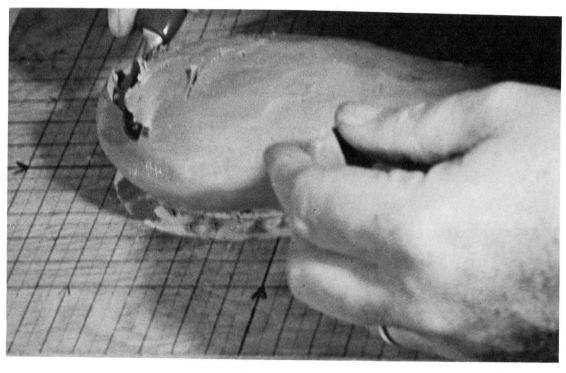

FIGURE 84. Cutting the flat area for the head seat.

FIGURE 85. Measuring how far back the tip of the bill will be.

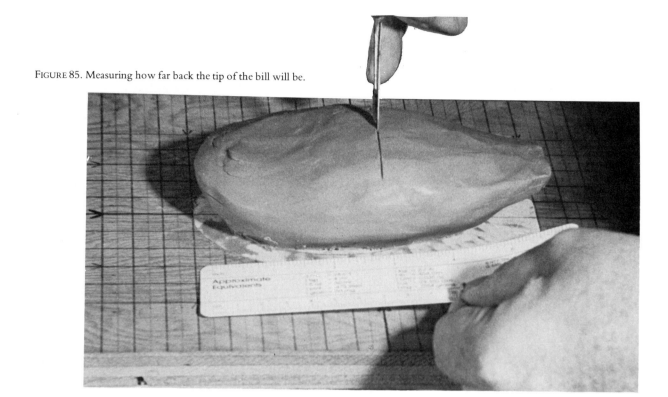

FIGURE 85. Measuring how far back the tip of the bill will be.

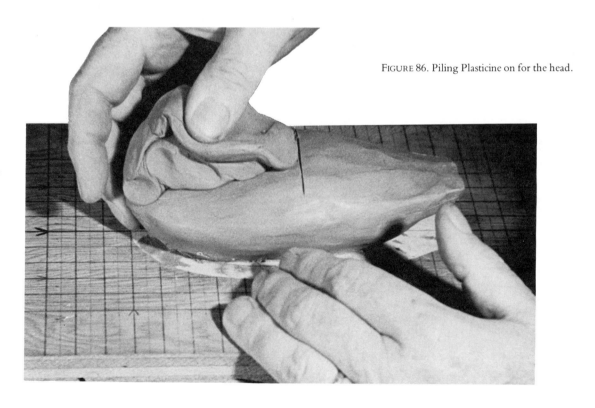

FIGURE 86. Piling Plasticine on for the head.

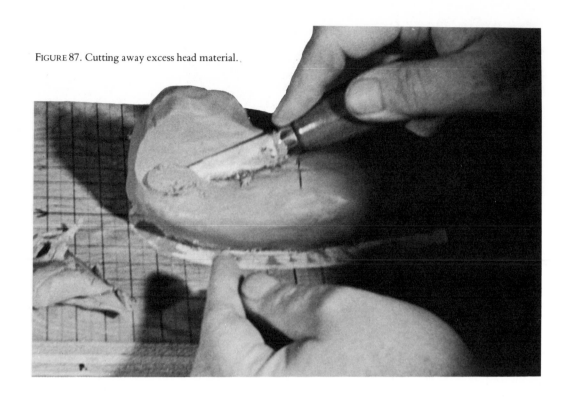

FIGURE 87. Cutting away excess head material.

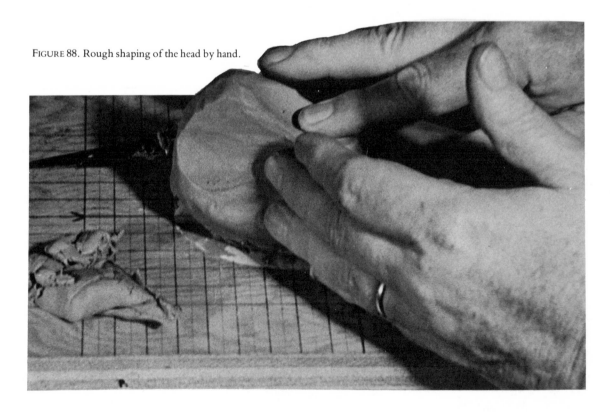

FIGURE 88. Rough shaping of the head by hand.

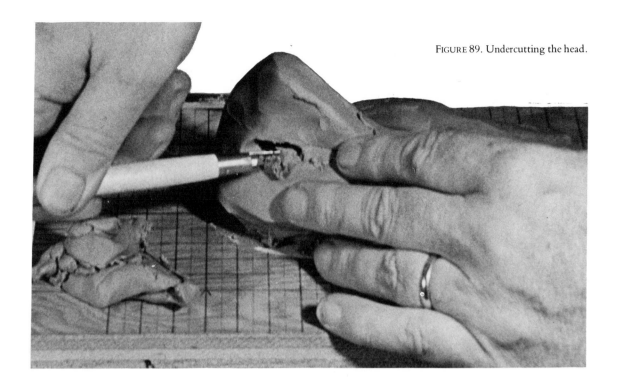

FIGURE 89. Undercutting the head.

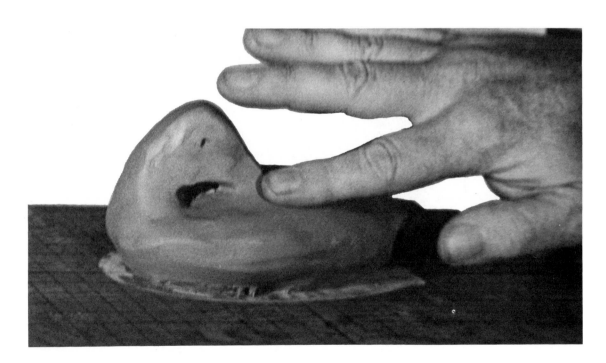

FIGURE 90. Final smoothing with fingertips.

55

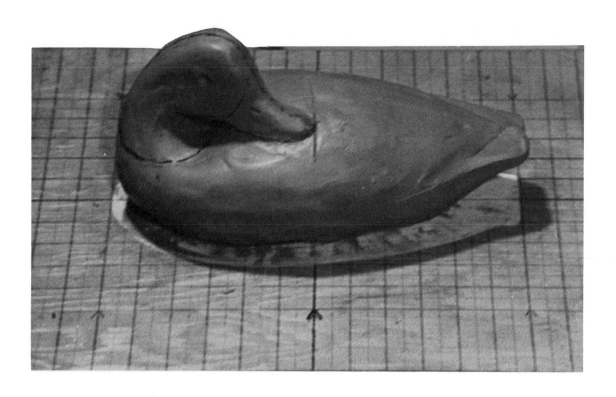

FIGURES 91, 92. The final form with the pattern lines of the head inscribed.

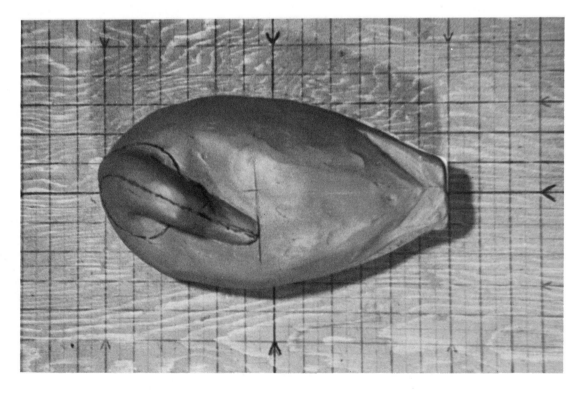

The proportions look good, so the patterns may be used. The whole process of sculpting this duck took me about ten minutes. I decided to do modeling about two years ago after working long and hard on a preening black duck for which I had drawn the usual two-dimensional patterns only to find the primaries were all wrong. A quick clay model straightened it all out. The great advantage in working Plasticine is the speed with which you change the form of it so that by trial and error you get just the shape you want. It also helps to have the half-size duck in front of you when you get to actually working in wood.

Because I have been encouraging you to make your own decoy designs, I would like to take the liberty of using a couple of my own designs to prove that any of us can plan and make a decoy. FIGURE 93 shows the patterns for a hollow canvasback, and FIGURES 94, 95, and 96 show the end result—quite stylized and with very simple painting. In FIGURE 97 are the patterns for the hollow black duck as finished in FIGURES 98, 99, and 100 and the same duck as adapted to a preening pose is shown in FIGURES 101, 102, and 103.

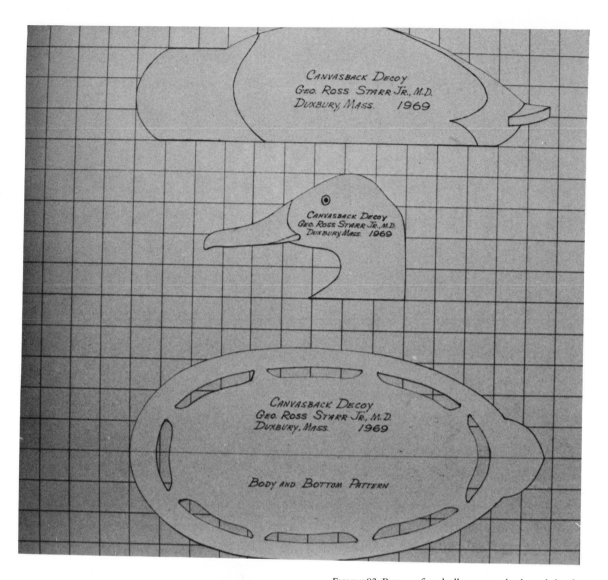

Inside the top pattern:
CANVASBACK DECOY
GEO. ROSS STARR JR., M.D.
DUXBURY, MASS.   1969

CANVASBACK DECOY
GEO. ROSS STARR JR., M.D.
DUXBURY, MASS. 1969

CANVASBACK DECOY
GEO. ROSS STARR JR., M.D.
DUXBURY, MASS.   1969

BODY AND BOTTOM PATTERN

FIGURE 93. Patterns for a hollow canvasback made by the author.

Fig. 94

Fig. 95

FIGURES 94, 95, 96. The completed canvasback made by the author.

Fig. 96

FIGURE 97. Patterns for a black duck made by the author.

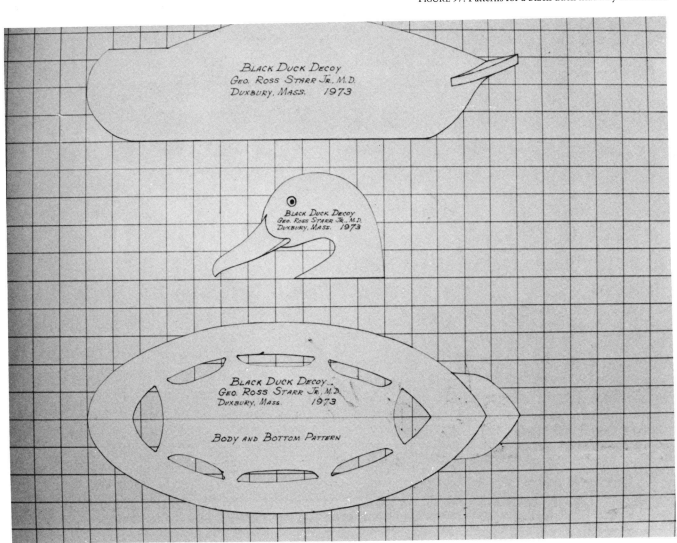

59

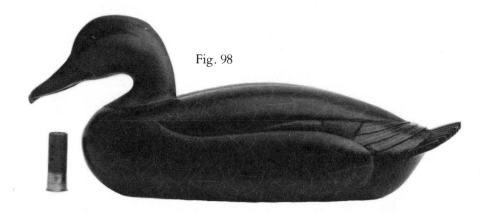

Fig. 98

Fig. 99

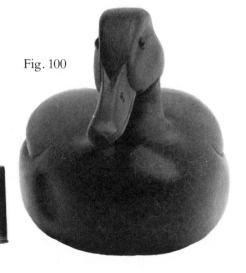

Fig. 100

FIGURES 98, 99, 100. The completed black duck made by the author.

Fig. 101

Fig. 102

FIGURES 101, 102, 103. The author's black duck, adapted to a preening pose.

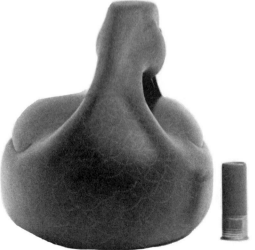

Fig. 103

CHAPTER 2

Materials

Before plunging into the actual making of a decoy, we must consider what material to choose and what tools are to be used in the fabrication. To someone who has not made decoys, the choice of material may seem unimportant, but this is not so. Before grabbing a hunk of wood and hacking away at it, there are several factors that have to be evaluated.

The first consideration is weight. On the premise that the stronger a carvable substance is, the more it will weigh, a line has to be drawn somewhere—otherwise the end product is going to be too heavy to handle easily. A lignum vitae decoy would be as strong as you could find—if you didn't mind that only the tip of the tail and the top of the head showed above water. Because of this we can eliminate the hardwoods from the materials' list. The second factor is ruggedness—the ability to stand up despite being tossed into boats and stacked in sheds and the awful toll that ice can wreak on a decoy. We must keep in mind, however, that a very soft material that shows deep nicks when anything hits it may not be worth the effort that has to be put into it. Next, the degree of ease with which the material can be shaped and carved must be considered. For instance, redwood is fairly easy to carve but its great tendency to splinter can negate all the work already invested.

Although it is not used as much as it might be if it were more easily obtained and cost less, basswood is almost the ideal carving wood. The grain is very fine and close—almost homogeneous—so that it carves like a hard cheese without any worry at all about grain. Most lumberyards do not carry bass regularly, but with some persistence you should be able to obtain some. It is especially good for heads and small work because it lends itself so well to detail carving.

The most common wood for decoys is pine. Northern white pine is a good carving wood and usually easy to obtain. If you get it locally, make sure it has been stored under cover long enough to be absolutely dry. The big disadvantage of this wood is the presence of many knots. If you can find it with only occasional small ones, it shouldn't make too much difference, but if it has a great many big knots, you will end up with too much waste. My own preference is for sugar pine. This is a pine variety that grows in Oregon and Washington and attains great height and diameter. The grain is very straight and fairly fine. The great thing about sugar is that it can run over 40 feet without a knot. Because of its clarity and easy workability, sugar is used a great deal for fancy millwork. Some of the better lumberyards stack it routinely, but if your favorite yard doesn't, they can order it for you. As with everything else in this world, the price of sugar has gone up. The last I got was $1.60 a board foot; however, its workability makes it well worth the price.

Cedar has always been a favored decoy wood in New England because it is strong and survives much better in water than many others. The type that was sought after is a variety known as swamp cedar, which grows only in swamps where there is water year around. As they get old and die off, swamp cedars stand out in the swamp like skeletons—curing and drying as the years go by to become fine decoy wood. The old decoy men didn't try to wade out and cut these trees in good weather but waited for winter when the swamp was locked in ice. It was relatively easy then to go out with saws and sledges and cut a whole year's supply of good decoy wood. I don't know personally of anyone who uses this method at the present time, but I'll be delighted to show you any number of good trees any time you want to try it. High ground cedar can be used, but it has much more of a tendency to splinter.

Balsa is a very soft wood that enjoyed quite a vogue for awhile as decoy body material. During World War II, the Navy used thousands of balsa life rafts. They were about 8 × 10 feet in size and consisted of an outer frame of balsa covered by waterproof canvas with a canvas "deck" stretched across the opening. The frame was about 15 inches square in cross section, made up of a large number of board feet of selected balsa all nicely glued up. When the war was finally over, these rafts, along with a million other items, were dumped on the market as surplus at very low prices. Decoy makers got word of this windfall and began stocking up. By 1948, the Ward Brothers of Crisfield, Maryland, had a yard full of rafts and were turning out balsa bodies on most of their birds. At the same time, Ted Mulliken, in Saybrook, Connecticut, who started and ran the original Wildfowler Decoys Co. was advertising decoys with balsa bodies made from rafts. Fortunately, the vogue died quickly, because balsa has more disadvantages than advantages. It is admittedly one of the lightest of woods, but it is not easy to carve. It requires extremely sharp tools and still has an awful tendency to "shred," that is, not cut cleanly. My own view is that balsa's greatest disadvantage is its porosity. As long as the surface of a balsa decoy is well-sealed and watertight, everything goes well. However, under the surface balsa has a very sneaky resemblance to a sponge. Once water gets an entry, it keeps on soaking in, and every ounce of water that accumulates adds to the weight of the decoy. The net result is that it floats lower and lower in the water and becomes that much heavier to lug home.

One Friday night in 1975, at the Waterfowl Festival in Easton, Maryland, a group of us were sitting in our room with the door open, just gabbing away about decoys, when George Walker wandered in with a decoy under his arm. It was a canvasback drake with a balsa body and a pine head—carved but unfinished. I held it and liked it and we made a deal. I was to pick it up on Sunday when the show closed and he had finished the bird. I went to see his carving display on Saturday and George said, "Hey, Doc, you want stickup primaries on that can?" More than a little nonplussed, I answered, "Sure, if you think they ought to be there." When George smiles you can never be sure what is coming next. "Don't worry, you old Scotsman, it won't cost you nothin' extra." As a Scot, I was quite naturally relieved—but intrigued.

When I went around on Sunday, George handed me the bird as you see it in FIGURES 104, 105, and 106. Obviously, I was more than pleased as I held this decoy with the primaries proudly sticking out from under the coverts. But I couldn't keep my big mouth shut. "He's beautiful, George, but what in the world are those primaries?" Again that smile. "You ought to know, Doc, you use them all the time—they're tongue depressors." It is still my favorite can decoy. On the other hand George and his son now make hollow pine decoys—so much for balsa. Like so many fine carvers, George always puts his "mark" on any decoy he personally carves—a purposeful fallacy that identifies his work. The small ellipse on the side of this can at the shoulder does not occur in nature, but George doesn't give a damn—it's his mark and he is proud of it, God bless him.

EIDER DRAKE *with a mussel in his mouth, carved by an unknown maker in Baileys Island, Maine. This represents the most simple and definitive form of decoy plumage-pattern painting – sharply outlined areas of black, white, and green. There is some old dark varnish on the mussel and lower bill.*

REDBREASTED MERGANSER *drake from the Monhegan Island – Penobscot Bay area of Maine. The flowing design of this bird is superb – a true example of the finest American primitive art. The plumage pattern is simple yet stylized. The colors were put on thin and flat with only a mild attempt to blend the red of the breast with the white above and below it.*

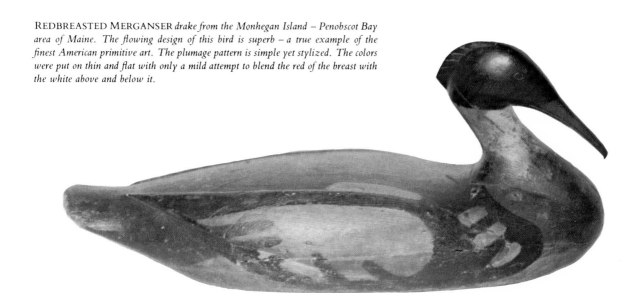

BLUEBILL DRAKE, *hollow, from the plans of Charles "Shang" Wheeler of Stratford, Connecticut. The overall paint pattern is quite simple and easily applied. Once the black undercoat on the back is thoroughly dry, the light gray coat is painted on and then scored by a graining comb to produce the wavy fine black lines across the back. The primaries, which in this case have been cut in very low relief, are shaded from a darkened ochre to burnt umber on the edges.*

AMERICAN MERGANSER *drake by "Buckeye Joe" Wooster of Ashley, Ohio, in 1975. This solid bird is more deeply feathered than the average working decoy and is beautifully done. All the colors are clear-cut and serve to outline the feathers. This gives an appearance of great intricacy, but is actually a fine illusion of shading because the excellent feather carving is what determines the overall effect. The only attempt at shading is the light gray stippling at the base of the tail and on the rear of the back between the primaries.*

WOOD DUCK *drake by Joe Lincoln of Accord, Massachusetts. Of particular note are the smooth lines and no-frills carving. Lincoln usually stuck to basic plumage patterns with well-defined areas of one color each with no blending. However, as seen in the detail, the sides of the wood duck demands a little more. These could not be left as a solid color. It was necessary to let them dry and then paint on the wavy black lines with a fairly dry fine brush.*

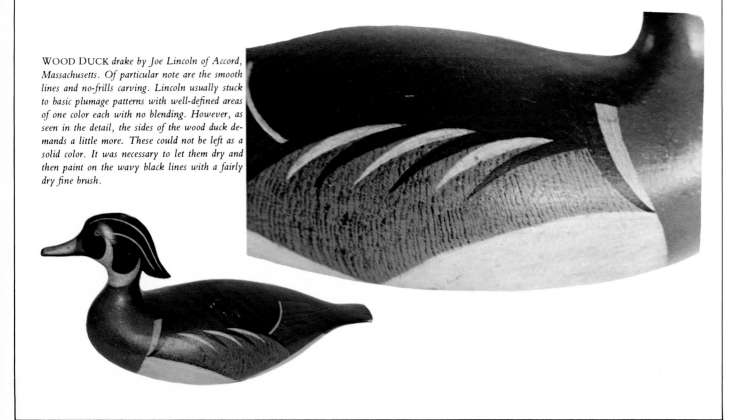

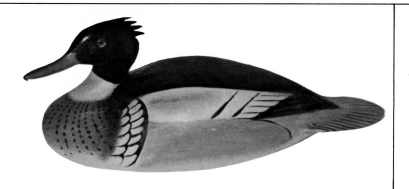

REDBREASTED MERGANSER *drake by Lem and Steve Ward of Crisfield, Maryland, about 1948. The body is made from balsa, which is very soft and porous. The paint pattern is quite definite but there is some degree of shading along the upper and lower sides and from the back down in front of the shoulder. The white of the underbody has also been blended into the red of the breast. This type of blending is best accomplished before either color has any time to dry. If one color is drier than the other, the blend tends to have a lumpy look.*

OLDSQUAW DRAKE *by Ken Harris of Woodville, New York. This solid decoy shows quite a bit more carving and painting than a working decoy really requires – especially the long vulnerable tail. In the detail picture you can see how the side panel was first outlined lightly in pencil and then painted with the darker gray. Each feather was then outlined in white using a fine brush and short strokes; then, using longer strokes with a drier brush, the white was blended into the gray.*

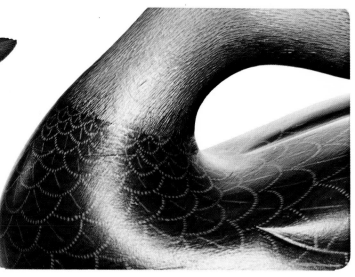

BLACK DUCK *by the author. This hollow decoy in the preening position is pure Stratford in style and execution with somewhat more feather carving than was usually used – just for the fun of it. From the close-up photo it can be seen that the body feathering is not difficult, but it is time-consuming. The head color – we are talking oil tube colors – is a mixture of yellow ochre and black with just enough thinner to make it spreadable. After it is applied, a sharp pencil is used to make the fine marks characteristic of a black duck head and to provide texture as against a simple flat surface. Again the fine brush is used to apply the rest of the black needed on the head.*

REDHEAD DRAKE, *a solid decoy made by A. Elmer Crowell of East Harwich, Massachusetts, in 1912. Crowell did more blending and obtained much softer plumage than just about any other professional maker of working decoys. I saw him at work painting in his shop – long after his arthritis would let him carve – and found he only used regular house paints right out of the can. These he put on in fairly definite daubs, waited just the right length of time, and then blended them with a soft dry brush, as on the back and flanks. The sides were painted off-white and, when almost dry, the black was lightly stippled on.*

CANVASBACK DRAKE *by George Walker of Chesterfield, New Jersey, 1975. This solid decoy has a balsa body and was painted with acrylics. The detail photo shows that the sides and back were painted light gray. After that, with his favorite #7 brush fanned out, George touched on the white, moving from front to rear. The same fanned-out brush was used to blend the black over the lighter side feathers.*

Fig. 104

Fig. 105

Fig. 106

FIGURES 104, 105, 106. Canvasback drake made in 1975 by
George Walker of Trenton, N.J. 16¼ × 7½ × 13⅛ × 6½ × 4⅜″

I would like at this point to talk a bit about the newest arrival on the decoy-making scene—the "burning iron." George used it on the head and the primaries. It is an electrical gadget used to burn pictures on flat wood surfaces that has now been adapted to put fine feathering marks on decoys. I have every respect in the world for the visual acuity of all members of the duck and goose families, but I do not really feel that they are capable of seeing "burned" marks on a decoy. The technique is fine for decorative carvings in the modern interpretation, but for actual working decoys, forget it.

Those of you who live along the Gulf Coast should not overlook the use of tupelo. I can't give you the names of any dealers who supply the butt cuts used in decoy making, but if you can make your way to any local carver, I'm sure he could steer you to a supply. Most Northerners don't think much of tupelo, but I have come to the conclusion that their thinking is a little awry. This last September I had the pleasure of being in New Orleans at the Louisiana Wildfowl Festival and saw some very fine carvings in this wood—and in great detail.

We have seen examples of cork decoys in FIGURES 16–18 and 19–21—one compressed and one natural. While natural cork, that is, slabs of cork tree bark in the same state as it is cut from the tree in the Mediterranean area, is still used for wine corks, fish floats, etc., it is pretty well passé as far as decoys are concerned. It was found that if cork was ground into small bits it could be mixed with a suitable adhesive and compressed into slabs of any desired size and thickness making it ideal for insulation. It didn't take long for the decoy crowd to get wind of this. However, it must be pointed out that compressed cork is made in several densities. The most dense is absolutely smooth with no little cavities between the bits and so is heavier and more expensive. Armstrong Cork Co. is the largest distributor of regular insulation-grade compressed cork and they happily have many local distributors. While compressed cork is produced in slabs from 1 to 12 inches in thickness and in varying lengths and widths, the most common thickness used for decoys is 4 inches. The material can be worked with a variety of files and rasps (including the Stanley Surform line) and sandpaper, the good old standby. Carvers differ in how fine or smooth a finish they like to get when working in cork—the rougher the finish the more "texture" and the less chance of reflection.

Larry Udell of Center Moriches made a rig of bluebills like the drake in FIGURES 107, 108, and 109. It is a fine working decoy with a rather rough rasped finish and is heavily painted in a very simple plumage pattern that is more than adequate for its job in life.

Fig. 107

Fig. 108

Fig. 109

FIGURES 107, 108, 109. Bluebill drake made by Larry Udell of Center Moriches, N.Y. 15¼ × 6¾ × 13 × 8 × 4″

F. C. Wilson of Tewksbury, Massachusetts, made the beautiful cork whistler (common goldeneye) drake (FIGURES 110, 111, and 112) in 1974. Normally a diving duck like the whistler rides with its tail low to the water, but if it tilts its head forward, its tail goes up. The entire aspect of this bird qualifies it for creative decoy design which, next to the actual making, is the second object of this book. The tail is an inset glued into the body. The body is glued to a ¼-inch plywood bottom board, and the wings are in high relief. The finish of the cork is quite smooth, with heavy base paint to fill in most of the small pits. Note the notches at each end of the keel on which to wind the anchor line.

From the beginning of this discussion with you I have tried to emphasize the importance of designing decoys to fit the demands of the areas in which they are to be used. By the early 1950s, after hunting with a wide variety of substandard decoys, I decided to make a set of working black ducks which I hoped would do a top job under the conditions we can expect to find in our local marshes here in Duxbury. In the first place, our tide varies from 8 to 13 feet, depending on the phase of the moon. The higher the tide, the more water has to come in and out of the marsh in a given time. At good full tides this can produce currents in the tidal rivers up to 4 knots, which can exert a great deal of drag on a decoy. Past experience of older gunners showed that in order to keep a decoy in position under those conditions and not have it drift up or down stream at least 16 feet of line and 2½ pounds of anchor per bird are required. This also takes into account the amount of wind we may have at the moment—if it's west, things aren't too bad; but if it's northeast, "Hang on, Mabel."

Fig. 110

Fig. 111

FIGURES 110, 111, 112. Whistler (common goldeneye) drake made in 1974 by F. C. Wilson of Tewksbury, Mass. $14 \times 6\frac{1}{4} \times 13 \times 7\frac{1}{2} \times 4\frac{1}{2}''$

Fig. 112

My gunning mate, Bud Nelson, went along with me on this plan, and we decided on twenty-four as the maximum rig with the idea that under varying conditions we could use from six decoys on up. I decided to use 4-inch cork plus a 1-inch bottom board so that they would "loom" up well and be visible from as far as possible. We finally decided on twelve regular heads: six feeders and six sleepers to give variety to the rig. One of the sleepers is shown in FIGURES 113, 114, and 115. I sanded the bodies as well as I could, but you will notice that the surface has a mottled look. Back in the 1940s, a man in Silverton, New Jersey, near Bay Head, ran into a substance called flock. This consists of very finely ground cloth fibers from which much of what we now call suede is actually made—a plastic plus an adhesive to which flock is attached electrostatically so that each tiny fiber stands on end. Well, anyway, this fellow found that if you put a very heavy coat of thick old dark paint on a cork decoy, patted on flock, let it all dry well, and then brushed off the excess, you came up with about as fine an imitation of the dull dusky brown of the black duck as you could hope to achieve. We used cotton flock—not nylon, which shines—one part black to two parts dark brown. The source of this material is the Ohio Flock-Cote Co. (13229 Shaw Avenue, East Cleveland, Ohio 44112). These decoys saw many years of hard usage before the flock coat began to wear off. The flock did a great job of protecting the cork from chipping.

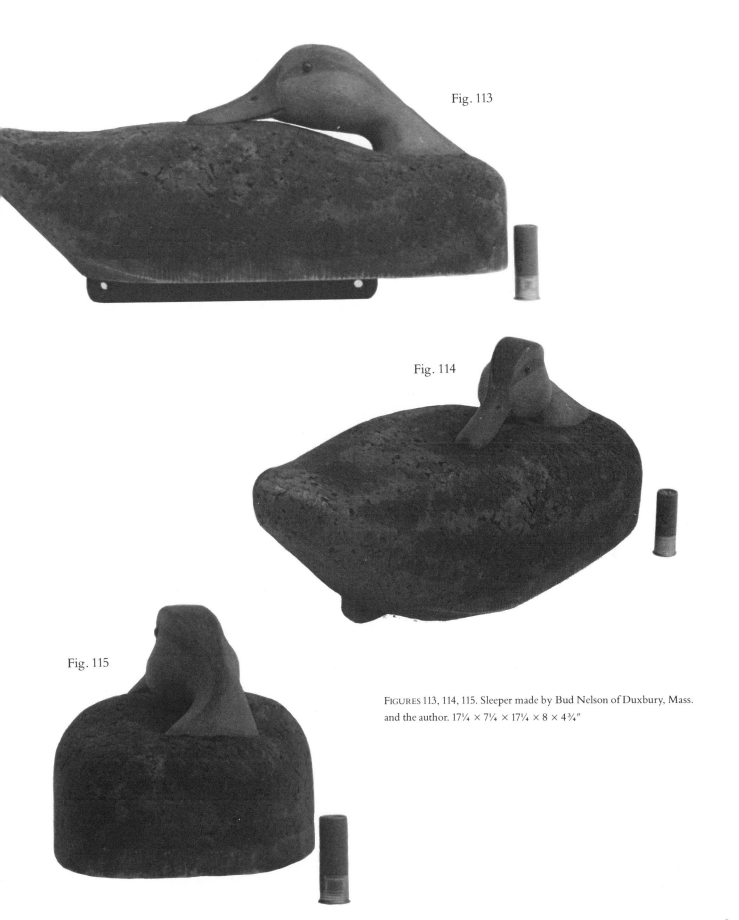

Fig. 113

Fig. 114

Fig. 115

FIGURES 113, 114, 115. Sleeper made by Bud Nelson of Duxbury, Mass. and the author. 17¼ × 7¼ × 17¼ × 8 × 4¾"

The short keel is not an accident or an oversight. We reasoned that with such a large bird, setting the anchor line abaft the bow might cause the decoy to swing or "swim" slowly from side to side and so give the idea of natural motion. It worked and we were very happy about it. Both cork and wood have a tendency to shrink to some extent over the years, so we fastened the heads on with galvanized lag bolts. Any sign of separation between the head and the body was corrected immediately by a quarter or half turn on the lag.

I must admit to being proud of this design because the decoys held up and worked well over many years. In 1953, I had a chance to get three very fine old decoys by Charles Hart of Gloucester, Massachusetts, for my collection. The owner of the birds at that time was Dr. Warren Babson, who was Chief of Surgery at Gloucester Hospital and is the owner of an excellent shooting area in the Essex marsh, just south of Hog Island. I was at his marsh at that time with Dr. Ham Hamilton, Chief of Surgery at Jordan Hospital in Plymouth, Massachusetts—my home base also. We argued around trying to arrive at a basis for trade, but were getting nowhere. What Warren really wanted was more good decoys. Ham, who had shot over my decoys, finally brought the deal to a close—a dozen cork blacks in trade for the three Harts. I am very happy to report that as of this last fall those corks are still in use and have graduated to being the preferred decoys. This should be the future for any well-designed and well-made decoy.

As a true Scot, I abhor waste whether it be wood or whisky. Before making any final decoy plans, find out in what dimensions the wood you desire to use is supplied. Remember also that if you are buying finished lumber—i.e., planed smooth on all sides—the dimensions so glibly rattled off by the lumbermen cannot be taken literally. In the modern lexicon a "1-inch board" never measures more than 13/16 inch in thickness. Two "2-inch planks" will never yield a decoy body more than 3½ inches in thickness. Once in a while you will run into a yard where they quote thickness in "quarters" or, more completely, "quarters of an inch." This usually applies to special finished woods like sugar pine. Under these circumstances "12 quarter" stock will measure a full 3 inches. Width is equally important. If your plans call for 6 inches and the only wood near it is 2 × 8 inches, think a minute. For every running or linear foot of this dimension that you buy, you must figure to waste a 2 × 2 × 12-inch piece. That amounts to a third of a board foot and at, let's say, $1.60 a foot, that's about 53¢ down the drain. Either that or you have an awful lot more keels than you have decoys. If they don't have 6 inch, try for 12 and split it. Lumberyards are pretty addicted to selling in even lengths—usually, 6, 8, 10, 12, etc., feet. Length then becomes another factor. If you design a body 13 inches long, try for a 10-footer (120 inches). Nine times 13 equals 117—leaving 3 inches for saw cuts and no waste. So now you want to know a little bit about decoy heads (which you will see in Chapter 4 laid out on a fine piece of sugar pine plank). If you haven't actually hunted ducks, you cannot imagine how fat and chubby their heads are when they are alive. This may seem more than a little silly to you, but make sure to design heads with good fat cheeks. It will make the whole decoy look better, whether flying birds can tell the difference or not.

Fig. 116

Many years ago in Chatham, Massachusetts, I bought an old goose who was preening its breast. In 1970, I decided to try one in this position, but using my own plans (FIGURES 116, 117, and 118). It is somewhat oversize and is hollow. The body is made of three slabs of 3 × 12 sugar pine. Another piece was used for the head and neck, and the base of the neck is mortised into the body in the Maine fashion.

The earliest decoys either didn't have eyes at all or they were just painted on. At some point carvers started using glass eyes that were made for the taxidermy trade. I'm not at all sure that wild birds can tell the difference, but certainly no one nowadays would make a decoy without them. In case you haven't yet seen them, duck eyes come in pairs and are formed by glass blowers at each end of a wire about 4 inches long. In the best grade eyes both the pupil and iris are blown of the proper color glass for whatever species you want to make. Also available are clear glass eyes with black pupils, and it is no great trick to paint the backs of them with whatever color you need for any given bird. Eyes are sold in millimeter sizes from 1 mm. for tiny miniatures up to more than 40 mm. for swordfish eyes and the like. I have always used 8 mm. eyes for regular-size decoys, but others recommend the 10 and 11 mm. sizes, which to me make the bird appear a little "pop-eyed."

This might be a good place to list a few of the companies from which eyes, paints, weights, and anchors and tools may be obtained. This is far from a complete list—just a few of the places I have dealt with over the years. Herter's, Inc. of Waseca, Minnesota 56093, has a fine catalog and stocks most everything. Woodcraft

Fig. 117

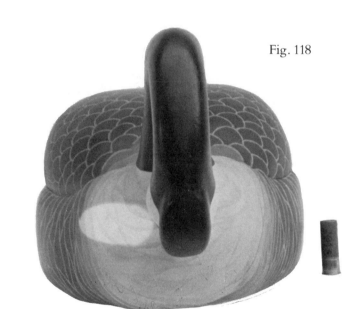

Fig. 118

FIGURES 116, 117, 118. Goose in preening position made in 1970 by the author. 29¼ × 10¾ × 24 × 12 × 8½"

Supply Corp. (313 Montvale Avenue, Woburn, Massachusetts 01801) also has a fine catalog that lists about every tool you can imagine—and many you can't. A relative newcomer is The Carver's Tree (Box 312, Island Lake, Illinois 60042), whose catalog specifically states that they carry what the wildlife carver needs. At many of the decoy shows and festivals you will meet a smiling fellow named George Walker, who has often proven his ability, as with the canvasback in FIGURE 104. When he isn't running around the countryside, he is the proprietor of the Chesterfield Craft Shop (Box 208, Chesterfield, Trenton, New Jersey 08620). George works through the shows and is never too busy to answer a question or show you a little trick of carving or painting that will save you time and make the whole job more fun.

FIGURE 119. Black duck head made in Stratford, Conn.

After you have done your carving and assembling, you will be looking at a very naked bird, and something will have to be done about that—which means paint. Until recently, the only answer was oil-base paints and they were nothing to sneer at. Since no live bird really has a shiny finish, neither should a decoy. It used to be possible at any art shop to buy what were called Japan colors. These were oil colors that were ground in a medium that let them dry absolutely flat with no shine at all. However, Japan drier is still readily available. By using this substance to mix and thin regular oil colors, you can end up with a very acceptable flat finish. Parker Paints (Box 433, Green Bay, Wisconsin 54305) still sells paint kits for decoys. They have a very flat finish and come in color sets with correct amounts of paints to do a dozen of any species of decoy you wish. Oil colors had a disadvantage we never realized in years gone by because there was really nothing we could do about it—they were slow to dry, which made it difficult to paint a decoy in one sitting. Oil colors require that the wood be painted with a sealing base coat first for them to get a proper grip and last.

Some years ago a line of acrylic paints became available and most of the decoy people shifted over to them almost immediately. They do not need a primer and sealer coat, but if you want a base coat it can be acrylic. Another great feature of acrylics is the fact that they are water soluble, which means no smell of turpentine around the house and that palettes and brushes can be quickly cleaned in soap and water. The best feature of acrylics is that they dry so rapidly—five minutes or so. This means that you can paint one color on a decoy and by the time you get the brush cleaned you can use that area as a handhold while you paint the next one. Once in a while this quick-dry feature is not the best thing. Down in Stratford, Connecticut, they developed a technique that gave more "texture" to black duck heads and bluebill topsides. FIGURE 119 shows a head done in that style. It is first painted black and allowed to dry thoroughly. The head color, a mixture of yellow ochre and black, is made up thick from the tube colors and a minimum of oil, and this is applied to the entire head except the bill. While this is still wet, a fine pencil is used to incise the small feather marks down to the black base coat. Two or three days later, when the whole thing is really dry, the top of the head and the "eyebrows" are done in black with a very fine brush.

CHAPTER 3

Tools

W HEN IT COMES TO TOOLS for decoy making, there are no hard and fast rules. Any gadget that will do the job is more than acceptable. It must be admitted that in the old days power tools were not available to the average decoy maker. You can be a pioneer, if you wish, but I for one am willing to use any power tool that will do the job. To make a few decoys, it isn't necessary to go out and buy a complete tool shop, because someone in the neighborhood is sure to have a pretty good shop—there are more amateur wood butchers in any given area than you would imagine. The key tool for decoys is the band saw, with which you can block out the body and cut out the heads with the least amount of work. If you don't believe me, try doing it with jig or coping saws. A drill press is great to use if you plan to make hollow decoys. A table saw can be a help, but an ordinary handsaw can do all the same functions, albeit at a slower pace and with more effort.

Probably the oldest method of making decoy bodies is to rough them out with a hatchet. FIGURES 120 and 121 show how this is done using a finely honed lathing hatchet. It took a lot of practice to do a good job and since I haven't had the practice and feel that there are better ways to get this wood off, I quit with these two pictures. With any tool but the hatchet, the piece to be worked must be held down securely, since the other tools all require two hands to operate. Because you have to work from various angles, it should be possible to quickly change the position of

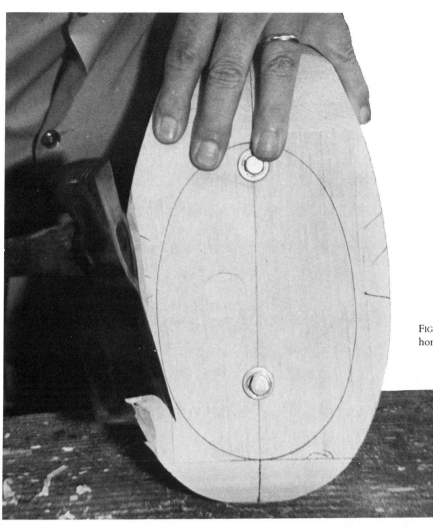

FIGURES 120, 121. Making decoy bodies using a finely honed lathing hatchet.

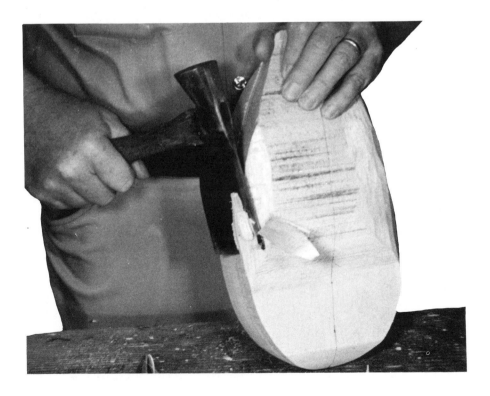

79

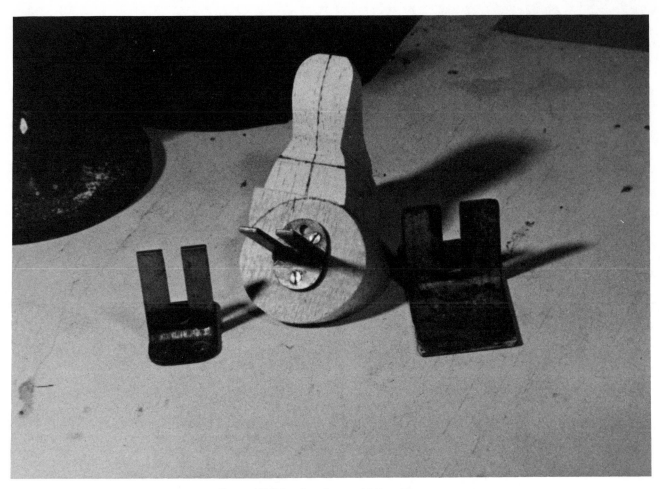

FIGURE 122. T-brackets for use with PoweRarm.

the piece. Any one of the various types of bench vises can be used to hold the work, but I did not use a vise in this series of photos because a block of wood in a vise does not make for clear overall photography.

Many years ago, a very charming man named Paul Schafer, from Gary, Indiana, arrived at one of the decoy shows with a crazy-looking gizmo called a PoweRarm. It was made by the company he worked for and was sold in lots of fifty or a hundred, to be used in the assembly of television sets and the like. Paul told me he got the idea that the PoweRarm was just what the decoy maker needed, and he made an arrangement with his company to do the missionary work in the field. From then on, Paul could be found at all the shows happily demonstrating and selling his wonderful machine. It will hold anything you attach to it firmly in any position you want, and will be seen in many of the following photos. The larger size, and the only one worth buying, in my opinion, comes in two varieties—mechanical control and hydraulic. The mechanical type is a simple cam lever and can be changed much faster than the hydraulic. When I got mine years ago, the T-brackets were of a different design—like the one on the right in FIGURE 122, which measures 2 × 4 inches. I soon found that this was too big for mounting smaller birds and heads and had a friend make up a few in smaller sizes. They make the tool much more useful. Incidentally, there seems to be some variation of the price on this tool from one catalog to another, so do a little shopping around before you buy.

Another very old-fashioned way of holding work was the shaving horse or shaving bench, illustrated in use on page 111. I had never seen one of these until about twenty-five years ago when I arrived in front of Sam Jester's shop in Chincoteague, Virginia, to find him sitting on one and carving a goose body. The pressure is applied by pushing forward on the foot pedal. Simply release this pressure and you can easily change the position of the piece and reclamp it. It is really fun to use, although it is no longer an everyday tool. The one pictured is very old, but unfortunately refinished, and was found in downstate Illinois.

Now that we finally have the work held fast, let's move on to tools used to shape it. The most commonly used tools are chisels and knives. I have never met anyone in a position to go out and buy a really complete set of carving chisels, which could run to well over a hundred items. Most of us start out with a small set and add on as the need for different-shaped chisels comes up in the course of carving. FIGURE 123 shows some of the chisels I have slowly accumulated over some forty years. They

FIGURE 123. Part of the author's collection of chisels, acquired over the years.

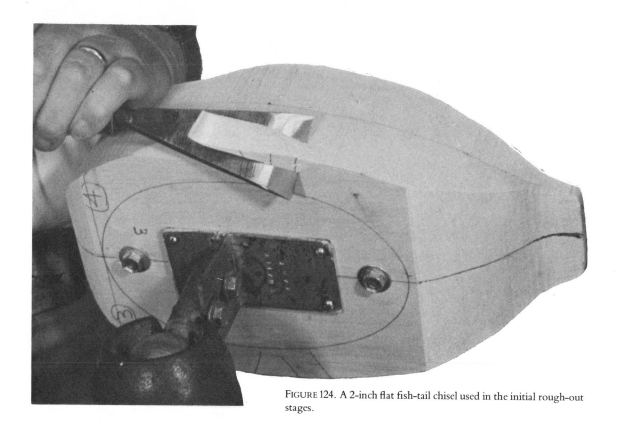

FIGURE 124. A 2-inch flat fish-tail chisel used in the initial rough-out stages.

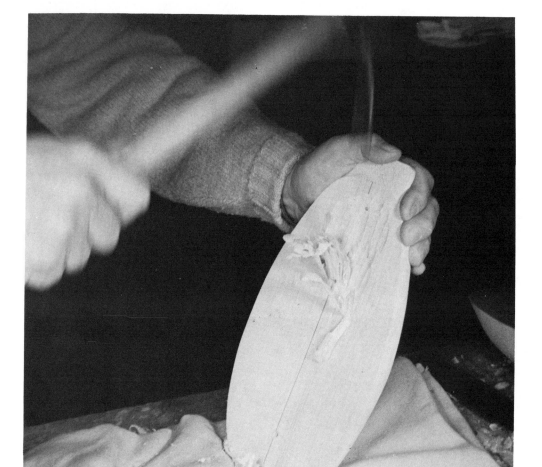

FIG. 125

represent most of the newer brands plus old ones from flea markets and antique shops. The big one in the middle is a 2-inch flat fish tail which I ground down thin on both sides. It is used in the initial rough-out stages, as shown in FIGURE 124. The small chisels used in the feathering process will be shown in Chapter 7. One very special chisel is known in New Jersey as a "dugout gouge" and can be a great help in hollowing any decoy body. The one shown in FIGURES 125 and 126 was hand forged many years ago by Somers Headley's father in Somers Point, New Jersey, and is 14 inches long. It looks like a very lethal tool, but in practice it isn't. The handle length and the curve of the gouge mean it to be used with wrist motion only, which gives great control over the cutting accuracy—and you can see what absolutely hellish speed it gives to the head.

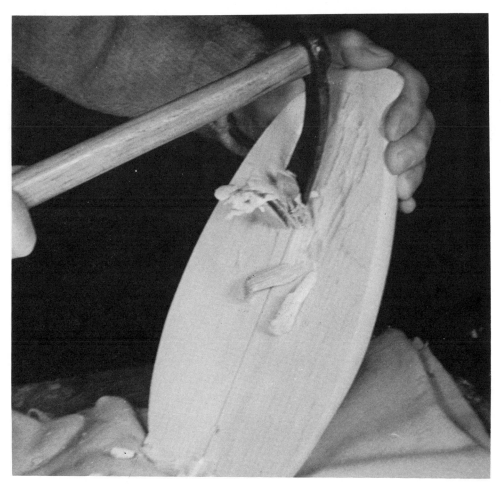

FIGURES 125, 126. A hand-forged dugout gouge chisel, made by Somers Headley's father of Somers Point, N.J.

FIGURE 127. Part of the author's collection of carving knives.

Carving knives also seem to just accumulate over the years and can run from a simple jackknife on up. Shown in FIGURE 127 are some of the ones I like and use. The best advice is to try them all and then decide what works best for you. There is always an opportunity for a great discussion when someone brings up the problem of sharpening knives. Woodcraft Supply alone lists six pages of sharpening wheels and stones, so I have no intention of going into all the theories of sharpening at this point. However, I have arrived at a method that keeps my knives and chisels sharp and myself happy. I use a 10-inch flannel buffing wheel at 3450 r.p.m. with a red cutting rouge until the edge is formed, followed by a very fine chrome rouge down to a final finish. These "rouges" or "compounds" and the big wheels can be bought from professional suppliers listed in the Yellow Pages under "Abrasives."

The best tool for removing large amounts of wood and for rough shaping in a hurry is a draw knife. Because of the long and hopefully very sharp blade, this can be a very dangerous piece of equipment and should always be handled with extreme care. The one shown in use in these photos is a vintage model I picked up at a country auction in New Hampshire back in the 1930s, but it is very fine carbon steel and takes a razor edge. For the smoothest cuts and best control of depth of cut, always hold a draw knife with the smooth side (unbevelled) up. After the heavy work with the draw knife, the next step is the spoke shave, which acts as a small two-handed plane. This last fall in New Orleans, I watched Richard Waquespak of Bayou Lafourche demonstrate his carving. He had no vise of any sort, so he roughed out the bodies with a hatchet. Next he used a spoke shave with the left handle cut off. By holding the body up against him firmly with his left hand, he finished the body using the spoke shave as a one-handed plane. I tried it and it works fine on tupelo but is not so easy to maneuver on the more common, harder decoy woods. Anyway, it's fun to meet a man who can be called an "inventive cuss."

If any more shaping is needed before the final smoothing, it is usually done with rasps and files. These are still used, but the Stanley line of Surform planes, files, or shaping tools (whatever name you wish to use) has proven to be extremely fine. They come in a variety of shapes and sizes and are particularly useful in bringing a rough-cut surface down to where it can be finished with sandpaper. The round file is particularly useful in shaping the rear end of the bird under the tail. The use of all these tools can be better understood from the pictures from here on than they can from my trying to describe them.

The newest great advance in carving aids is a very powerful and versatile flexible shaft tool made by the Foredom Electric Co. If you are not in too much of a hurry to make a decoy, smaller and more reasonably priced flexible shaft outfits are available, but don't push them beyond their capacity. The virtuoso of the Foredom is the aforementioned George Walker, who dispenses them from the Chesterfield Craft Shop. The Foredom people make fourteen different handpieces, including those nasty ones at a 45-degree angle used by dentists, and it is pretty obvious that the decoy maker doesn't need all this hardware. George recommends the basic machine as shown in FIGURE 128, including the #44 handpiece which takes ¼-inch shafts and the #30 with a Jacobs chuck, which handles all diameter shafts from nothing to ⁵/₃₂ inch—which covers just about every shaft size you will ever need. The canvasback in FIGURE 104 was over 90 percent formed by George with this machine. If you don't believe me, just watch George at the next decoy show. For carving and sanding, this tool can make every man an expert after a little practice.

When you are a carver, you learn to keep your eyes open for any new techniques and equipment that might come along. Six years ago I was gamming with Bob Clifford in Dennis, on Cape Cod, when he showed me a gadget that looked like a fiddle bow but had emery cloth in place of the horsehair used to play fiddles. Bob

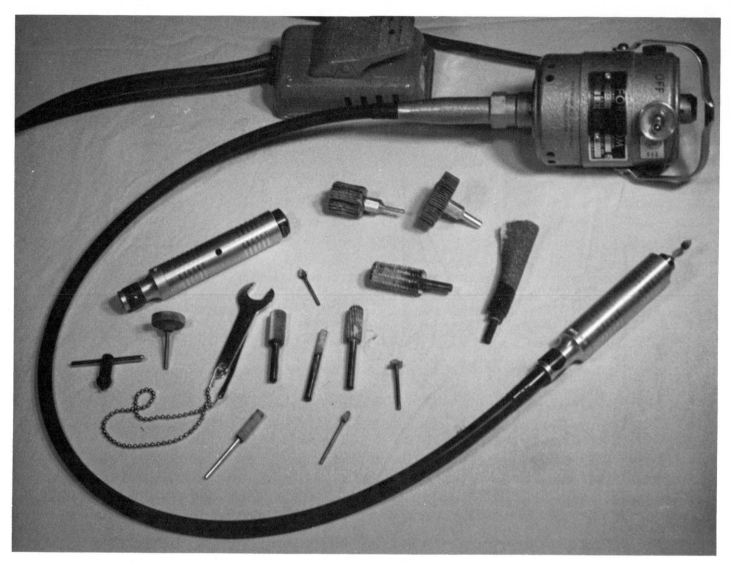

FIGURE 128. Basic Foredom machine with chucks and tools.

didn't know who invented it, but he said it was the greatest sanding aid he had ever seen. He very nicely gave me one to take home and try. After using it for awhile, I started on some tries at redesigning and came up with the one shown in FIGURE 129 and in use in later photos. The grid is 1 inch square. The depth of the throat has been increased to 2⅜ inches. The pistol grip turned out to be the most comfortable and the tension on the bow can be controlled by the middle finger. The length depended on the fact that belts for belt sanders are obtainable in 36-inch lengths and half of this gives us just the length we need. You can buy belts of different grits—from coarse to fine—and simply slice them to the width you desire. I cut them from ½- to 1¼-inch wide × 18 inches long. After some disastrous experiments with alligator clips to hold the belts on, I finally settled for Moore pushpins, which can be put in and pulled out easily. The bow itself is made of ¾-inch plywood. I made one with a throat depth of 6 inches, which works great for sanding the throats of decoy heads without getting hung up on the bill.

In FIGURES 55–57 there is a bluebill hen by D. K. Mitchell which shows feathers that were hammered into the surface with specially designed tools. Many years back, Ben Schmidt made himself some feather cutters from rounded steel bar stock (FIGURE 130). A different feather size and shape has been ground into each end. These were loaned to me by Dr. Ed Bowman of Grosse Point Farms, Michigan, who many years ago was given them by Ben. The method of using them is shown in FIGURES 131 and 132, which are self-explanatory.

After Shang Wheeler died, Charlie Disbrow came into possession of the jig shown in FIGURES 133 and 134. When making solid decoys, it is common to run a dowel from the bottom of the bird to almost the top of the head. Holding the head and body in just the position you want them while drilling the dowel hole presents a pretty tricky problem. Shang invented this holder to solve the problem. Note the inset piece of surgical felt to protect the head from scarring. The circle and cross on the bottom (FIGURE 134) show where the hole would be drilled.

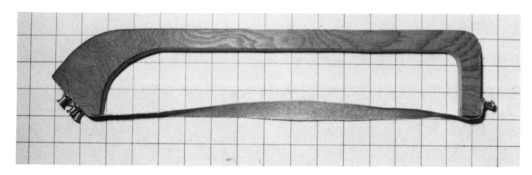

FIGURE 129. A sanding tool designed by the author, based on a design by Bob Clifford, of Dennis, Mass.

FIGURE 130. Feather cutters made by Ben Schmidt of Centerline, Mich., from rounded steel bar stock.

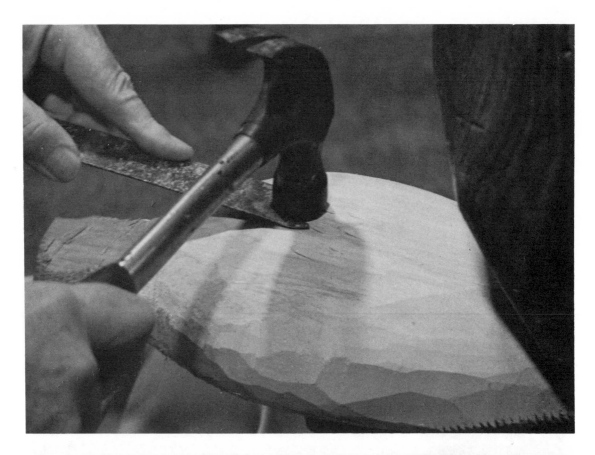

FIGURES 131, 132. Ben Schmidt's feather cutters in use.

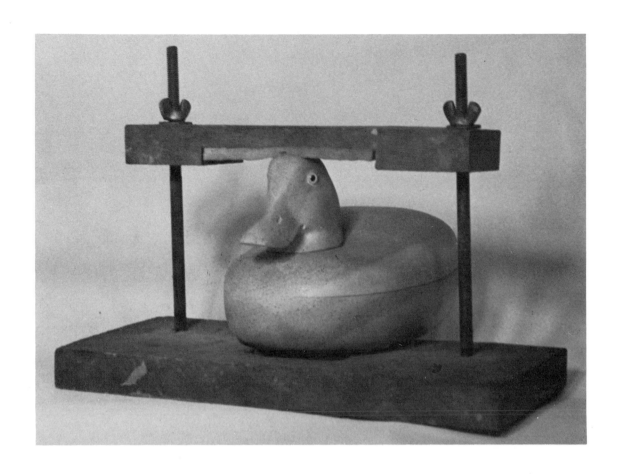

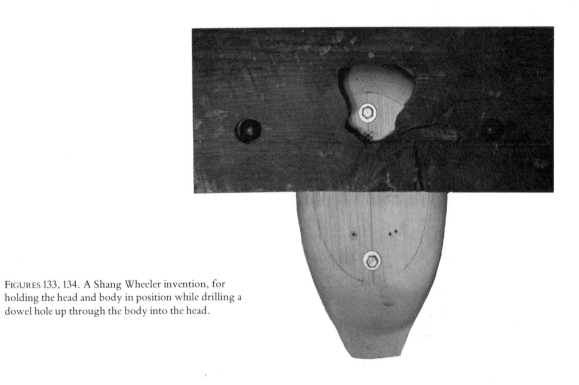

FIGURES 133, 134. A Shang Wheeler invention, for
holding the head and body in position while drilling a
dowel hole up through the body into the head.

CHAPTER 4

Layout

As a matter of actual fact, the care used in laying out and cutting the stock for decoys can make things a lot easier from there on in. This is particularly true when the body is to be fashioned from two layers. The first step is to establish a center line on the board to be used (FIGURE 135). This line should be drawn on both sides of the board, which in this case is 2 × 7 sugar pine. Patterns are then traced—top and bottom sections—being sure that all center lines are in order (FIGURE 136). About a half inch should be left between sections to allow for the saw cut. When the square is used to draw the cutting line (FIGURE 137), it should not be in the center but to one side to allow room for the saw kerf (FIGURE 138).

The next step is to cut off the body sections (FIGURE 139), which in this mechanical age is most easily done with a power saw. Once the sections are cut, they should be marked with randomly placed lines so that they can be reassembled for profile cutting once the body sections have been sawn out (FIGURE 140). In order to be able to correctly line up the two sections, it is necessary to carry the leading point of each section over to the edge of the plank and down the side (FIGURES 141 and 142). Before cutting out the body sections, it is well to number the body and the corresponding side sections as shown in FIGURE 143, so they will line up properly for cutting the profile. The completely cut body sections should look like FIGURE 144. To continue along the way to accurate alignment, the top and bottom center

FIGURE 135. The first step in laying out and cutting the stock for a decoy: establishing a center line on the board to be used.

FIGURE 136. Tracing the pattern.

FIGURE 137. Using a square to draw the cutting line.

FIGURE 138. The square used in drawing the cutting line should be to one side to allow for the saw kerf.

FIGURE 139. Cutting off the body sections with a power saw.

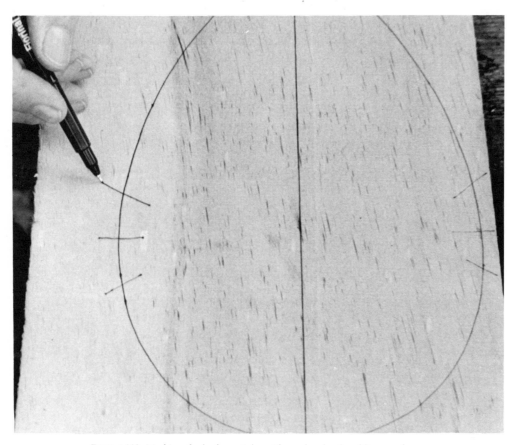

FIGURE 140. Marking the body sections with randomly placed lines so they can be reassembled later.

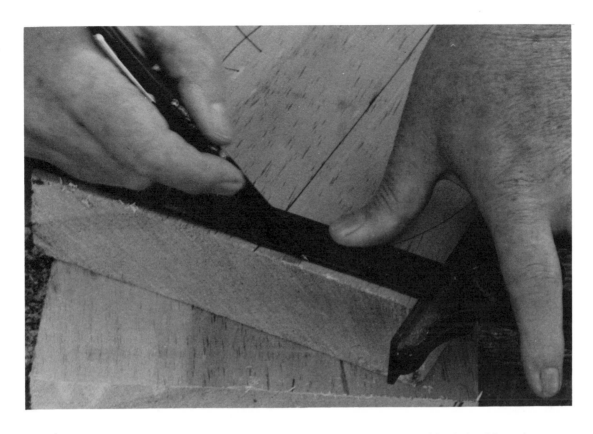

FIGURES 141, 142, 143. Carrying the leading point of each section over to the edge of the plank and down the side. Number the body and corresponding side sections so they will line up properly for cutting the profile.

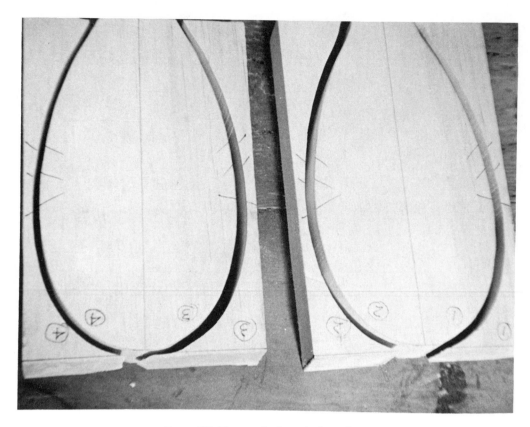

FIGURE 144. The completely cut body sections.

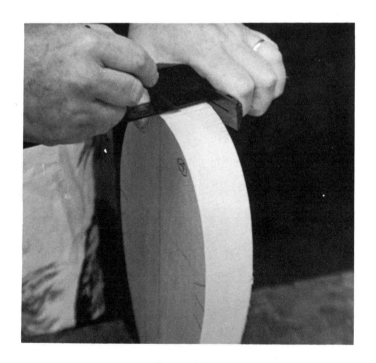

FIGURES 145, 146. Connecting the top and bottom center lines at the front and rear of the sections.

94

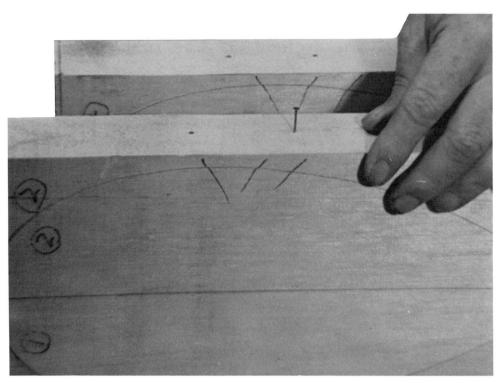

FIGURE 147. Nailing the side sections to the body.

FIGURE 148. Tracing the profile pattern on the block.

lines should be connected at the front and rear of the sections (FIGURES 145 and 146). The side sections should be nailed to the body as shown in FIGURE 147. Use small nails and only nail in the area of the guideline marks so they will not be in the way when the profile is cut.

Now line up the two sections using the guidelines from FIGURE 143 to assure that the top section lies directly over the bottom at the forward end. Lay the profile pattern in place as shown in FIGURE 148 and trace it on the block. Make a mark on the bottom section at the point that will mark the front end of the flat bottom area of the actual decoy (FIGURE 149), and from there carry a line across (FIGURE 150). Using this line, put the bottom pattern in place and trace it (FIGURE 151). The top and bottom must now be fastened together securely enough so that not only can the profile be cut but the decoy body itself can be carved. In this case, 2½ × ¼-inch lag screws were used. They must be positioned a reasonable distance apart while making sure that they do not protrude above the profile (FIGURE 152). Marking the bottom for the lag screws is shown in FIGURE 153. The metal gadget is a jig for

FIGURE 149. Marking the bottom section at the point that will mark the front end of the flat bottom area.

FIGURE 150. Carrying the line across from the flat bottom area.

FIGURE 151. Tracing the bottom pattern.

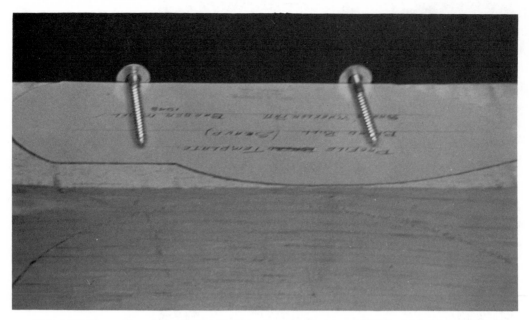

FIGURE 152. The position of lag screws used to fasten the top and bottom securely for cutting the profile and carving the body.

FIGURE 153. Marking the bottom for the lag screws.

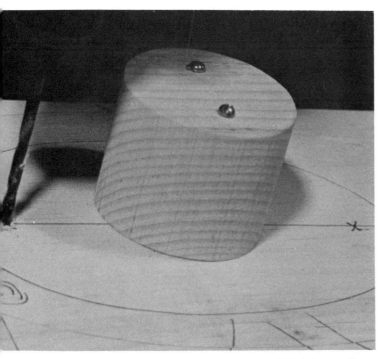

FIGURE 154. Round block screwed to bottom to hold body in an ordinary vise if PoweRarm is not used.

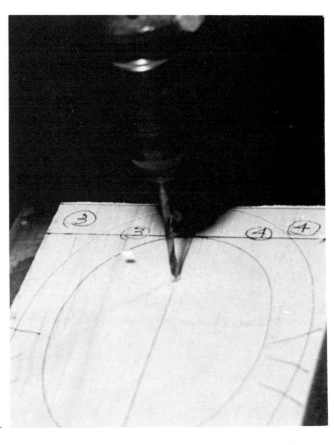

FIGURE 155. Drilling the lead holes for the lag screws.

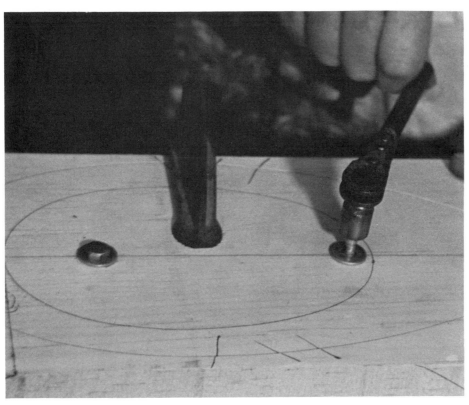

FIGURE 156. Clamping the body sections to a bench before setting in the lag screws.

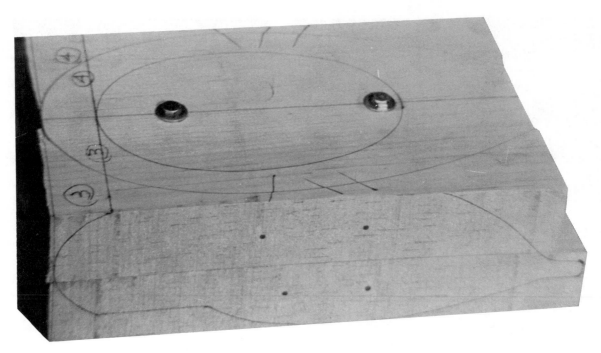

FIGURE 157. The block is now ready for the profile to be cut.

fastening the work to a PoweRarm. If the PoweRarm is not being used, room should be left for a block, which can be used to hold the work in most positions in an ordinary vise while the body is being shaped. Putting the whole body in and out of a vise repeatedly makes far too many dents. It is essential to drill the lead holes for the lag screws (FIGURE 155). A $^3/_{16}$-inch bit leaves enough side wall for the threads to get a good grip, but is not tight enough to cause splitting. Before setting in the lag screws, clamp the body sections to a bench so there will be no daylight between the body halves (FIGURE 156). In FIGURE 157 we see the block ready for the profile to be cut.

Unfortunately, most home bandsaws will not accommodate a 7-inch thick board with the upper saw guide in place. The saw shown in FIGURE 158 cutting the profile is a 14-inch Delta with the upper blade guide removed to give clearance for the 7-inch cut. This sawing step must be done very slowly and carefully so that the blade can maintain its correct alignment even without the guide in place. After the profile has been sawn, the side boards are removed (FIGURE 159). In FIGURE 160 we see the body completely sawn and ready for shaping. The guidelines are very important. The center line is self-explanatory. The line around the side marks the point of maximum beam to which you will shape from the top down and from the bottom pattern up.

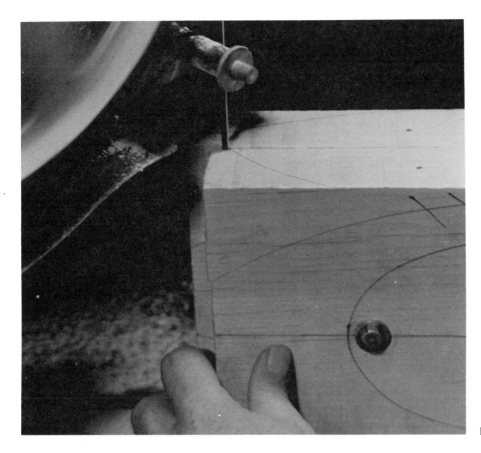

FIGURE 158. A 14-inch Delta saw cutting the profile.

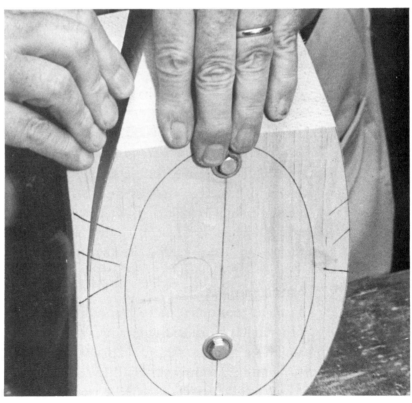

FIGURE 159. Removing the side boards
after the profile has been sawn.

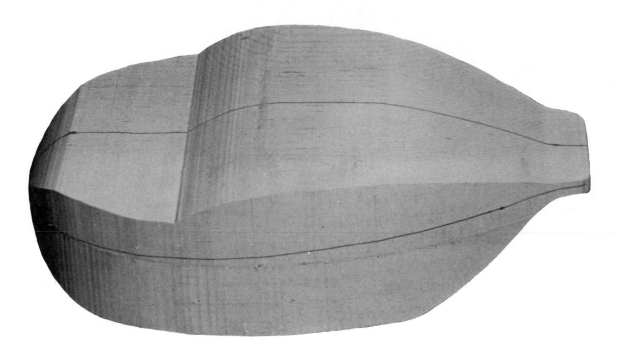

FIGURE 160. The body completely sawn and ready for shaping.

We now move on to laying out and tracing the head patterns on 2-inch stock. It is essential to have the grain of the wood running the length of the bill, not only for maximum strength, but to make the carving that much easier (FIGURE 161). Don't forget to "dot the eyes" (FIGURE 162)—a misplaced eye can spoil the whole look of the head. FIGURE 163 shows the process of cutting out the head; snugging the patterns in this tight makes the sawing a little trickier, but it sure saves wood. Personally, I like to have the eye position in view at all times while carving, so when the head block is cut, I drill a fine hole in the eye position all the way through (FIGURE 164). Nothing looks worse to me than a decoy head on which both eyes are not in the same position. This little hole takes care of that worry. FIGURE 165 shows the head cut and drilled.

Some men can take a block like the one above and start right off whittling away. Unfortunately, I'm the type who works somewhat by formula and so must have guidelines. FIGURES 166, 167, 168, and 169 show the guidelines I have worked out for my own use over the years. It follows that a center line completely dividing the head is the first step. I next make the cross lines to indicate the base of the bill on both its

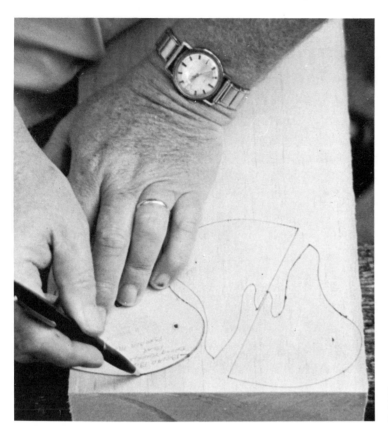

FIGURE 161. When tracing the head patterns on 2-inch stock, have the grain of the wood running the length of the bill.

FIGURE 162. "Dotting the eyes."

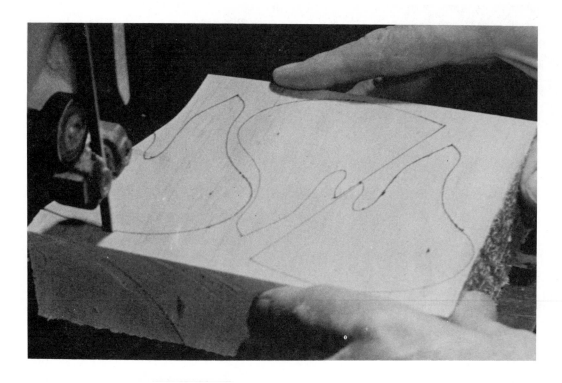

FIGURE 163. Cutting out the head.

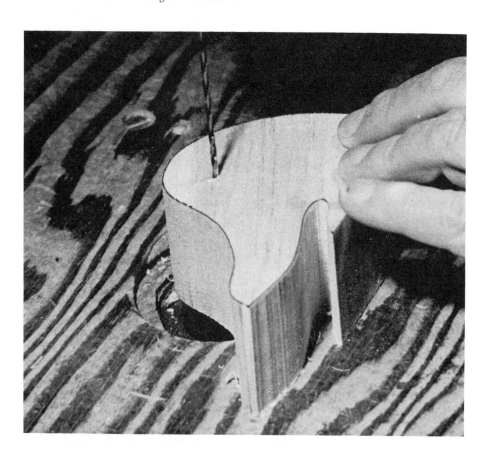

FIGURE 164. Drilling a fine hole in
the eye after the head block is cut.

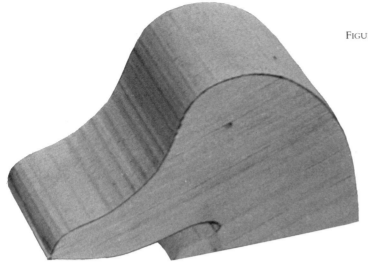

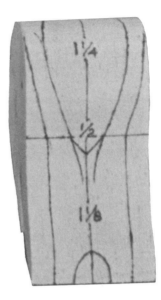

FIGURE 165. The head cut and drilled.

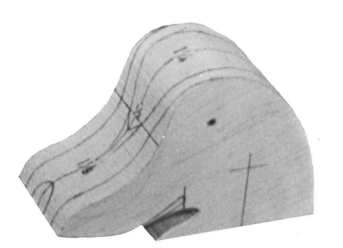

FIGURES 166, 167, 168, 169. Guidelines on the head block.

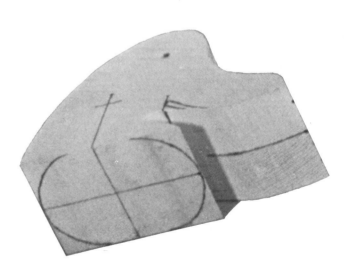

top and bottom. Next is the bill width—in this case 1⅛ inches. These lines are carried back and out to the widest part of the head. The notch where the head meets the bill is set here at a half inch and the lines are carried out and over the crown for the width of the top of the head and then taper back down to the neck. To me by far the most important mark is the cross on the side which is the point that will be the very widest part of the head—the cheeks—and which goes a long way to giving the head its real character. The base line is the center of the neck and the "cross"

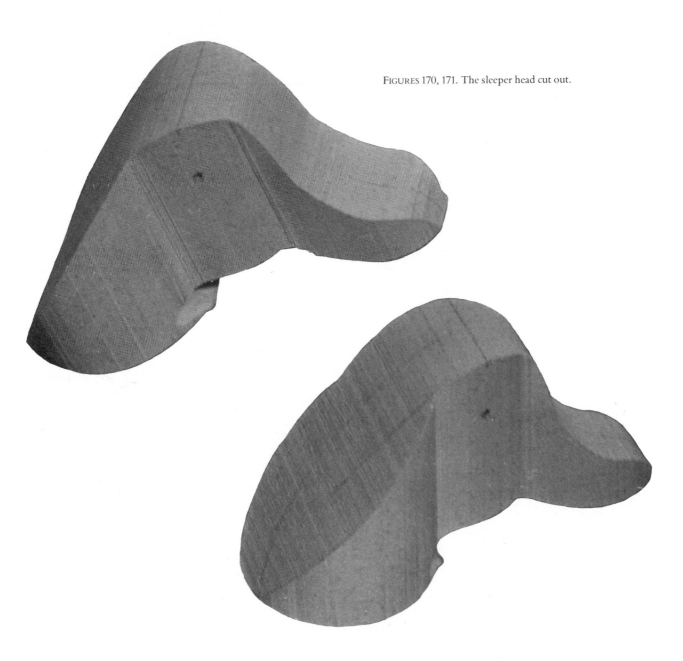

FIGURES 170, 171. The sleeper head cut out.

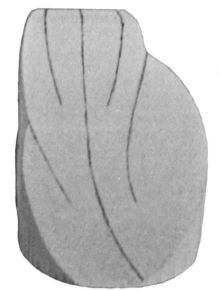

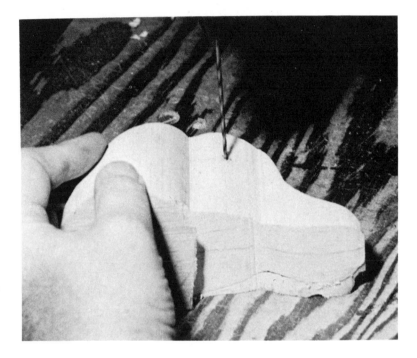

FIGURE 172. Curved lines coming down from the head to the base of the neck.

FIGURE 173. Drilling the eye holes.

represents a line from the tip of the bill back along the maxilla, or lower jaw, to the point where it joins the skull. The nib at the end of the bill should be marked to preserve the center line until the bill is all shaped.

FIGURES 170 and 171 show the sleeper head cut out. All the guidelines will be the same as for the straight head, except the necessary curved lines coming down from the head to the base of the neck where it blends into the body (FIGURE 172). Since the sleeper head is considerably wider than the straight, you can't be quite so chintzy with the lumber. When you lay it out, be sure the center line of the head is parallel to the edge of the stock, so that when it is cut out, you can use that outside slice as a jig for drilling the eye holes to make sure they are in the right position (FIGURE 173).

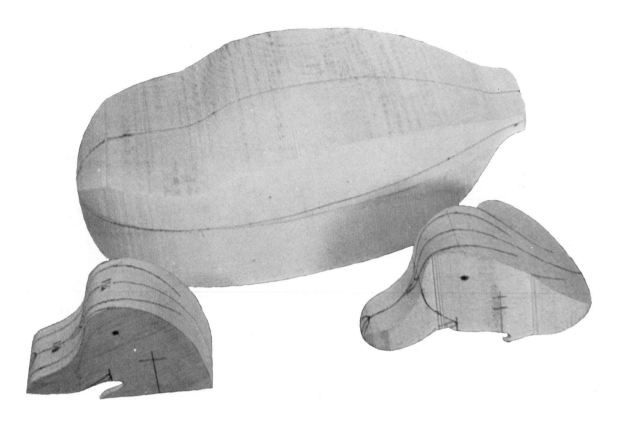

FIGURE 174. The body and the two heads cut out and marked.

FIGURES 175, 176. The pieces brought together.

108

FIGURE 174 shows the body and the two heads all cut out and marked. In FIGURES 175 and 176 the pieces are finally brought together and give promise of becoming decoys. Because the PoweRarm will be used as the holding device for much of the carving and painting, FIGURE 177 shows the proper way of fastening the holding jig to the block.

FIG. 176

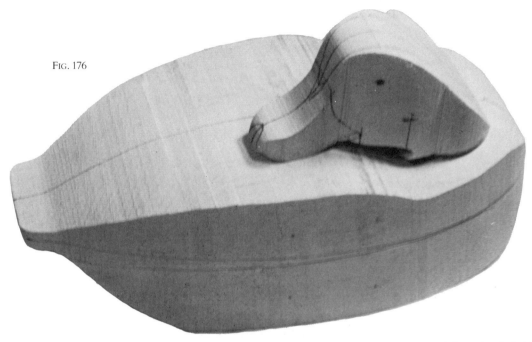

FIGURE 177. Fastening the holding jig to the block.

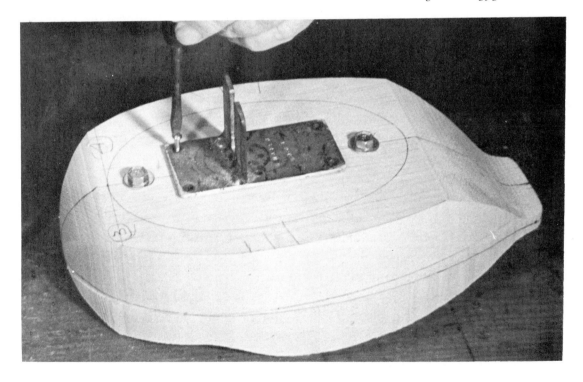

CHAPTER 5

Carving the Body

I F YOU HAVE STAYED WITH ME this far, you may well have gotten the feeling that we were never going to get beyond a lot of lecturing and a bit of band sawing, but that happy moment has finally arrived when we can finally begin hacking away with a clear conscience. I have no regrets about bringing you this long way around, because I sincerely believe that what we have covered is essential to a true understanding of the what and why of decoy making.

In an attempt to establish the fact that only I am responsible for the workmanship pictured herein, FIGURE 178 shows "himself" taking the early cuts on a decoy body using a draw knife and holding it on a shaving bench. Further steps in roughing are shown in FIGURES 179, 180, and 181. The cut being taken in FIGURE 182 demonstrates that with a bit of practice the draw knife can be used for rather fine shaving cuts and not only big grabs. FIGURE 183 shows the very rough-cut body.

FIGURES 184 and 185 show further work using the spoke shave. Note how the body shape is gradually being rounded to the guidelines. This tool allows finer controlled cuts. The name "spoke shave" is no accident—it was invented by wheelmakers for carving the spokes.

In the old days, a series of rasps and files would have been brought into play at this point. Those tools will still do a marvelous job, but nowadays just two shapes of Surform files—the flat and the round—will do the whole job very easily and well. In FIGURE 186 a flat file is used to complete the rounding of the body and FIGURE 187

FIGURE 178. The author taking the early cuts on a decoy body using a draw knife and holding it on a shaving bench.

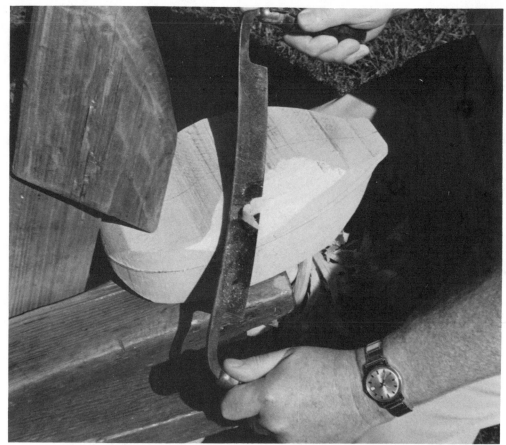

FIG. 179

FIGURES 179, 180, 181. Further steps in roughing.

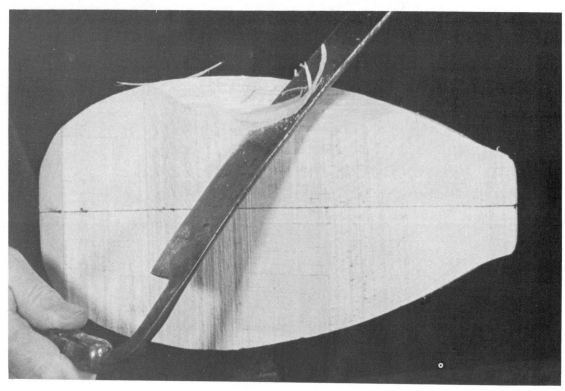

FIG. 180

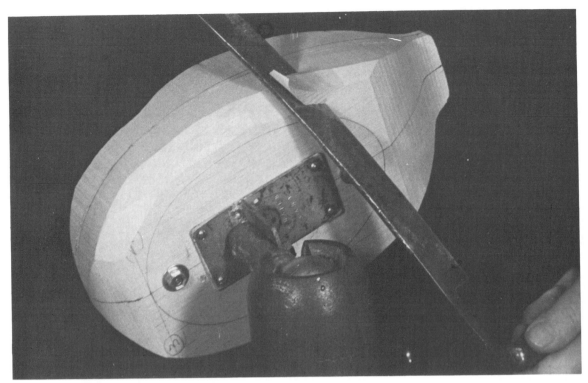

FIG. 181

FIGURE 182. The draw knife being used for cutting.

FIGURE 183. The very rough cut body.

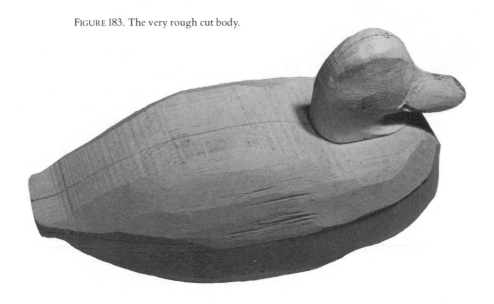

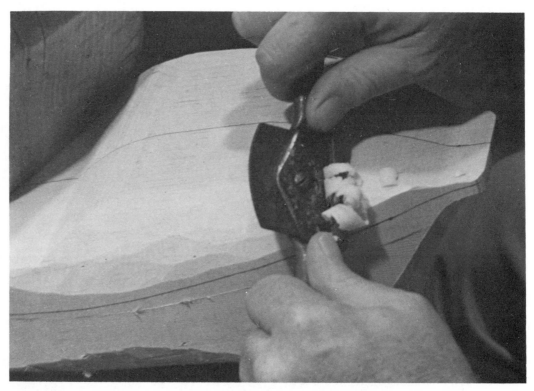

FIG. 184

FIGURES 184, 185. Further work using the spoke shave.

114

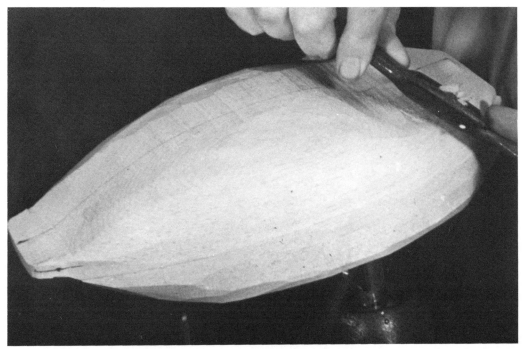

FIG. 185

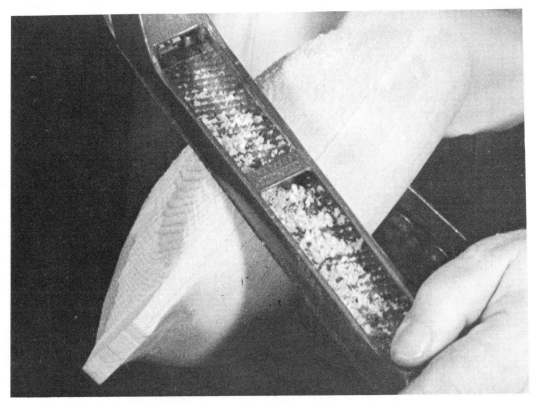

FIGURE 186. A flat file is used to complete the rounding of the body.

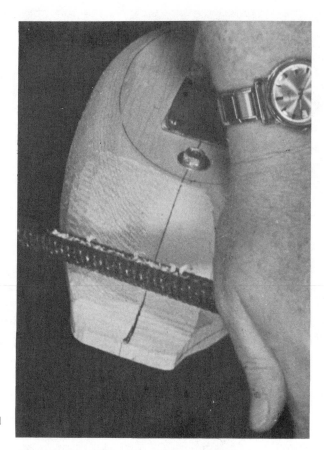

FIGURE 187. A round file, particularly helpful in cutting and rounding under the tail.

FIGURES 188, 189. A sanding bow in use, with a coarse grit for cutting away the file marks.

shows the round variety, which is particularly helpful in cutting and rounding under the tail.

With the shaping completed, there now remains the problem of sanding, which used to be the worst and longest chore of all. However, by using the sanding bow it becomes more fun than work. FIGURES 188 and 189 show the bow in use, with a coarse grit for cutting away the file marks. FIGURE 190 shows the body with the rough sanding completed.

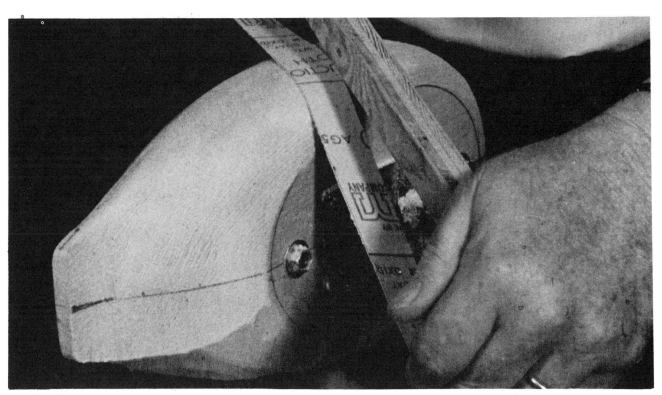

FIGURE 189

FIGURE 190. The body with the rough sanding completed.

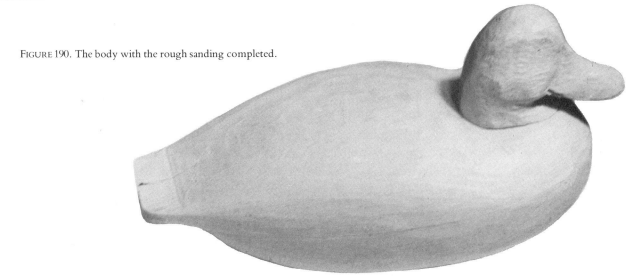

CHAPTER 6

Carving the Head

Now THAT WE HAVE SHOWN how easily and quickly the body can be made, we move along to the head carving, which is more complicated, but something anyone can do if you understand why certain cuts must be made and generally pay very close attention to what is going on. FIGURE 191 shows the start of removing the extra wood from either side of the bill with a skew chisel. Someone once asked Michelangelo how he did his marvelous sculptures. He replied that it was very simple: "I see the figure as I want it in the block of marble, and I simply cut away what doesn't belong there." It might be a good idea to glance ahead to FIGURE 228 and study what the completed head looks like so you will better understand how we are going to remove the extra wood to reveal the head buried inside.

FIGURE 192 shows removing the rest of the wood in to the bill line with a "fish tail chisel." In FIGURE 193, a shallow gouge is used to shape the side of the head and the top of the bill, and the process is carried on with a round Surform (FIGURE 194). In FIGURE 195, a broad shallow gouge is used to shape the back part of the head and to hollow the side of the neck below the "cross" on the cheek, which mark is preserved until the final sanding. FIGURE 196 shows the hollowing and rounding from the cheek to the back of the neck. Rounding the front of the neck under the throat is done with a small shallow gouge (FIGURES 197 and 198). The guidelines for the bill are redrawn in FIGURE 199 and a small gouge is used to begin the undercutting of the sides of the bill, since the lower jaw is narrower than the upper (FIGURE 200). In

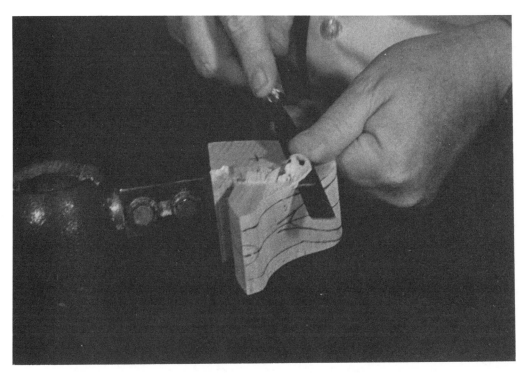

FIGURE 191. The start of removing the extra wood from either side of the bill with a skew chisel.

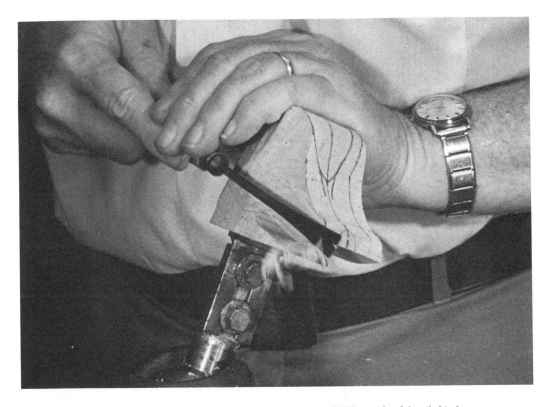

FIGURE 192. Removing the rest of the wood in to the bill line with a fish-tail chisel.

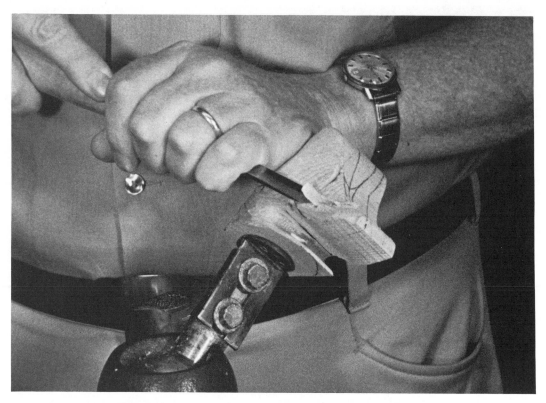

FIGURE 193. Shaping the side of the head and the top of the bill with a shallow gouge.

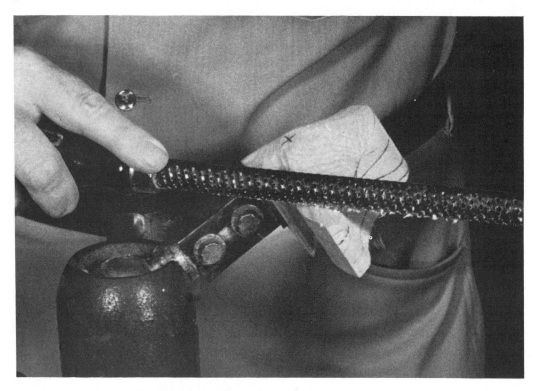

FIGURE 194. Further shaping with a round Surform.

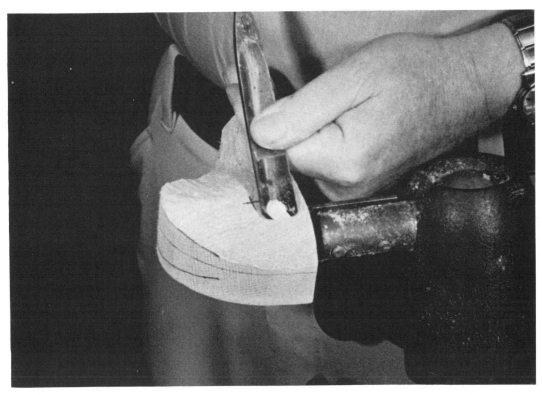

FIGURE 195. Shaping the back part of the head and hollowing the side of the neck with a broad shallow gouge.

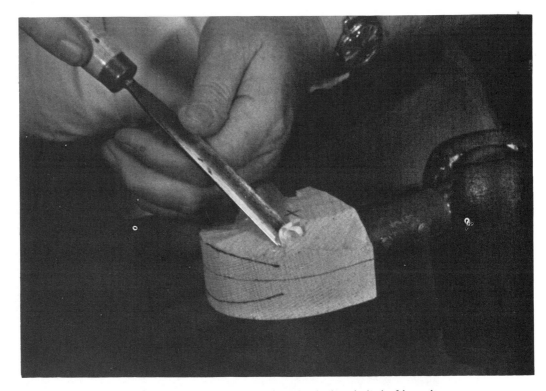

FIGURE 196. Hollowing and rounding from the cheek to the back of the neck.

121

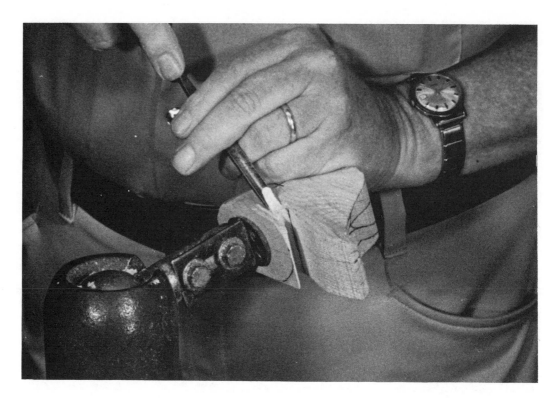

FIGURES 197, 198. Rounding the front of the neck under the throat with a small shallow gouge.

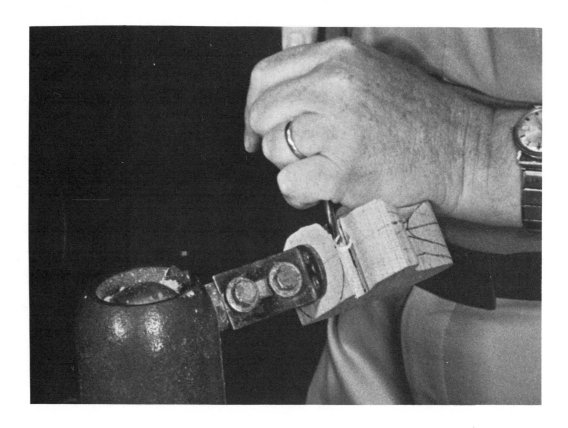

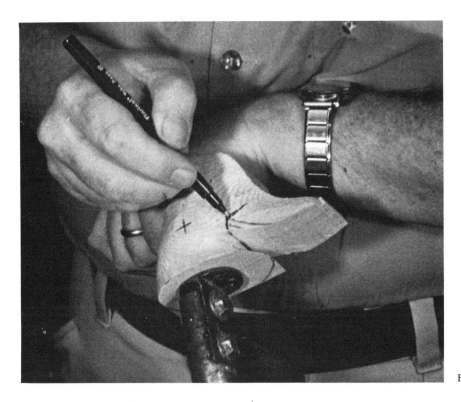

FIGURE 199. Redrawing the guidelines for the bill.

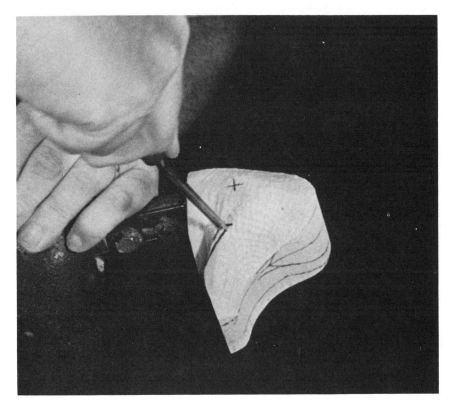

FIGURE 200. Using a small gouge to begin the undercutting of the sides of the bill.

FIGURE 201, the undercut is completed and a small "V" chisel is used to cut the line where the bill meets the head. A skew is then used to round the cheek forward to this line (FIGURE 202). The upper side of the bill is somewhat concave and this hollowing from the base line outward is shown in FIGURES 203 and 204. The outline of the nib should be cut quite deeply, after which the front end of the bill can be rounded off to its final shape (FIGURE 205). FIGURES 206 and 207 show the incising and cutting of the notch at the base of the bill.

Because so many people now have a Foredom tool or some similar flexible shaft arrangement, I want to show how the head can be carved with a power tool. It is obvious that the head block must be cut out and marked no matter what the method of carving. With power you can take more wood off faster and in a more controlled manner than is generally possible with chisels alone. The basic cutter is the rotary file, which is shown in action in FIGURES 208, 209, and 210 doing the rough work and throwing out a grand amount of wood dust. Cutters, like chisels, aren't necessarily bought in sets, but are acquired one at a time when you need a certain size or shape. The $7/16$-inch diameter cutter in FIGURE 211 makes a smoother and

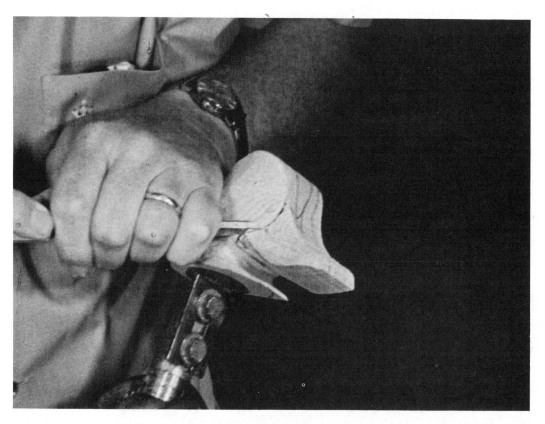

FIGURE 201. Cutting the line where the bill meets the head with a small V chisel.

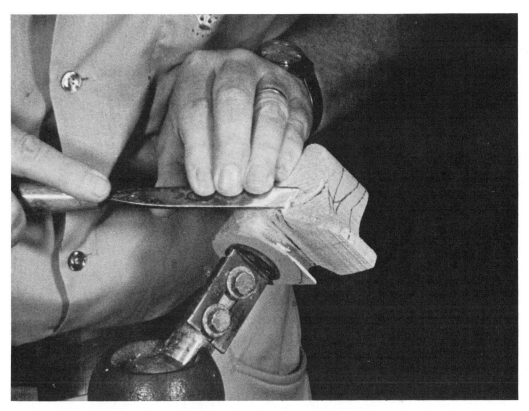

FIGURE 202. Rounding the cheek forward to the line where the bill meets the head with a skew.

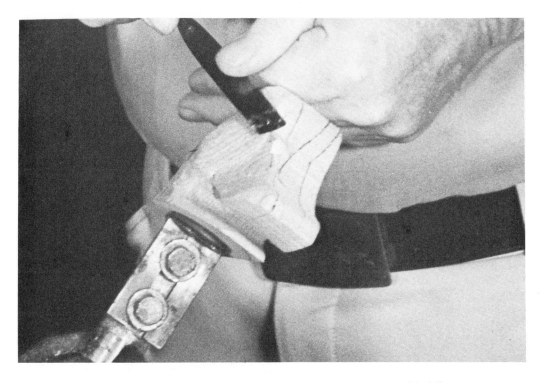

FIGURE 203. Hollowing from the base line outward on the upper side of the bill.

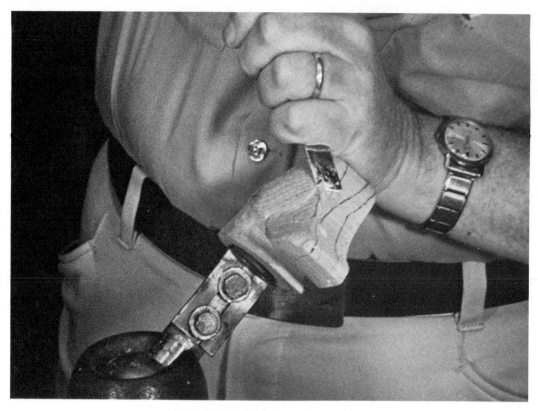

FIGURE 204. Completion of hollowing begun in Figure 203.

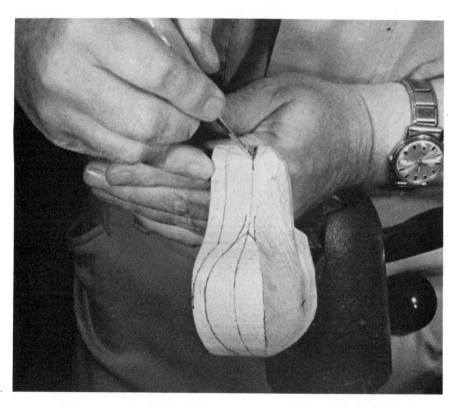

FIGURE 205. Cutting the outline of the nib.

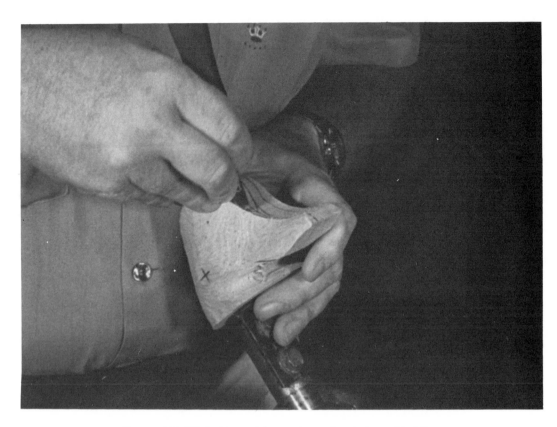

FIGURES 206, 207. Incising and cutting the notch at the base of the bill.

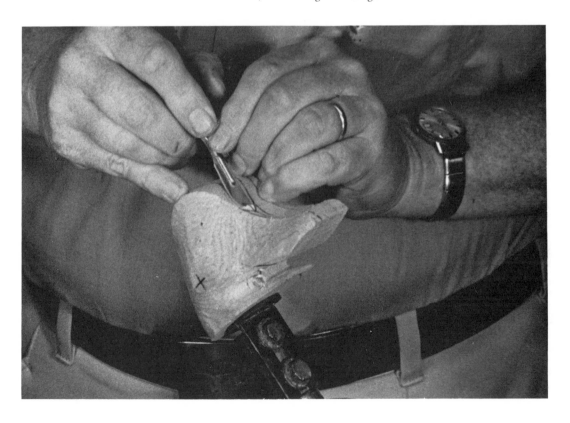

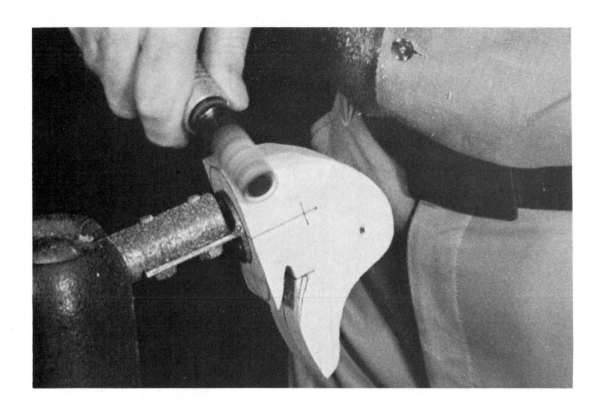

FIGURES 208, 209. Cutting out the head block with a rotary file.

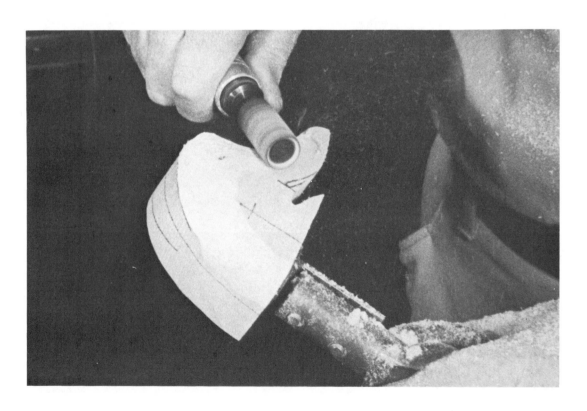

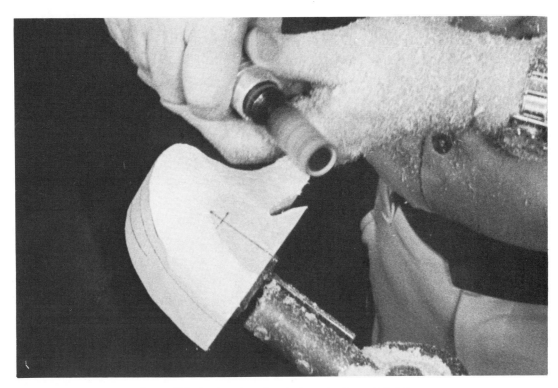

FIGURE 210. Continuation of work shown in Figures 208, 209.

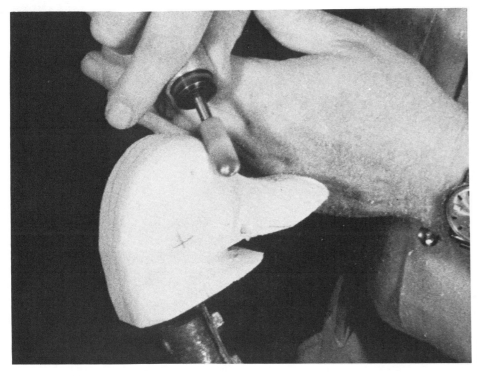

FIGURE 211. A ⁷⁄₁₆-inch diameter cutter makes a fine second-stage tool.

shallower cut than the rotary file and makes a fine second-stage tool. The handiest cutter for the close carving on heads is the ¼-inch size shown making the bill groove in FIGURE 212. It is then used to shape the bill (FIGURE 213) and to cut out around the nib (FIGURE 214). It is especially handy in cutting the underside of the bill and in rounding the neck in front (FIGURE 215). Note in FIGURE 212 that the cutting of the lower jaw is still best done with the small gouge and knives. No duck has a flat head, so it must be rounded off just a bit as in FIGURE 216.

Back to the sleeper head for just one moment. There are two big initial cuts to establish the curve in the neck. I find these easiest to do with a broad gouge as in FIGURES 217 and 218. From there on the carving is the same as for the regular head.

Sanding the carved head down to its final finish is somewhat less fun than sanding the body. It is possible to get some power help on the job, which can save a great deal of time. Among the accessories shown in FIGURE 128 are two small "flap" sanding wheels, each mounted on its own mandrel. These will do a pretty good job, but you must be very careful to prevent grooving from letting the edges of the wheels tilt and cut at an angle to the surface you want. George Walker noticed that the half-inch rotary file has a narrow slit down its length where the edges do not quite come together. He takes a 3-inch square section of a belt sander, shoves one corner into this slot, rolls it around, and fastens it with a small tough rubber ring or a length of plastic electrical tape, as on the one on the right in FIGURE 128. This

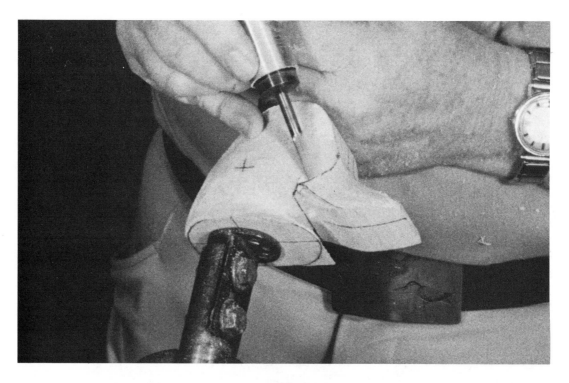

FIGURE 212. A ¼-inch diameter cutter making the bill groove.

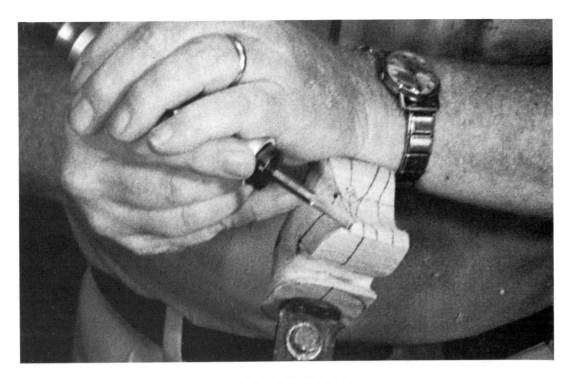

FIGURE 213. Shaping the bill with a ¼-inch diameter cutter.

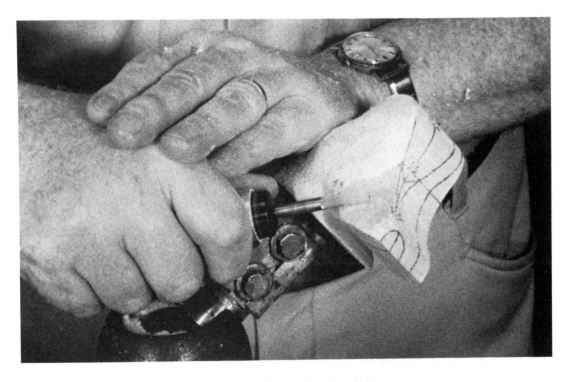

FIGURE 214. Cutting around the nib with a ¼-inch diameter cutter.

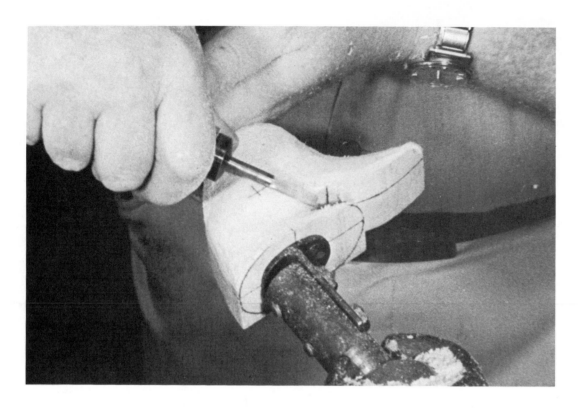

FIGURE 215. Cutting the underside of the bill and rounding the neck in front with a ¼-inch diameter cutter.

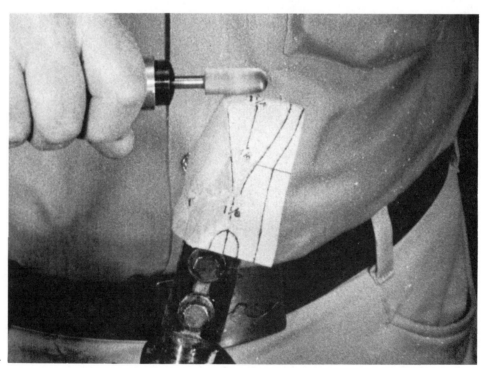

FIGURE 216. Rounding off the head.

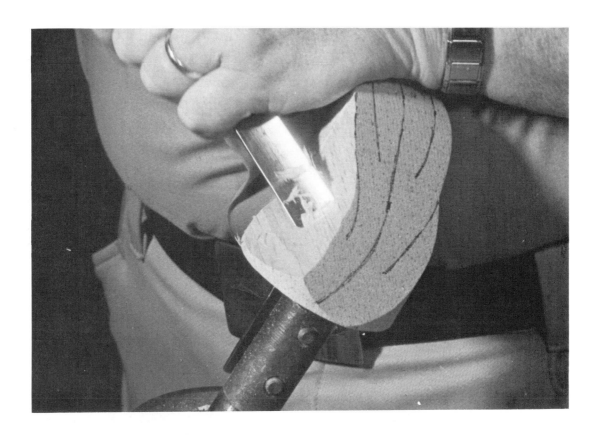

FIGURES 217, 218. Making the two big initial cuts to establish the curve in the neck with a broad gouge.

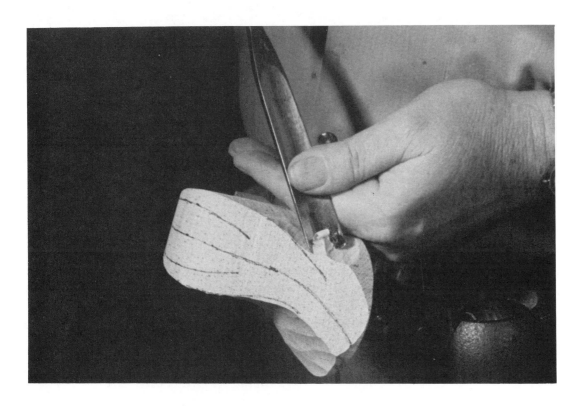

provides a flexible sanding drum about 2¼ inches long. This pretty well eliminates any tendency toward grooving. The one shown is a heavy grit and somewhat rigid. Finer grits will mold themselves to a greater degree and are truly amazing on concave as well as convex surfaces. Unfortunately, when you have gone as far as you can with these gadgets, there is only one way to do the rest of the job—hand sanding.

Now that the sanding job is over, we can add the final touches to the head. As in FIGURE 219, mark on the nostrils—for art's sake, make sure both sides match—and cut them using a very fine gouge (FIGURE 220). A very fine "V" gouge can be used to cut the groove which parallels the bottom of the bill (FIGURE 221). Using a small burr, cut the eye sockets (FIGURE 222), and test them for size by making sure the eye itself just fits (FIGURE 223). By far the best material for embedding the eyes so that they will never come out is a hand-moldable epoxy put out under the name of Epoxybond. It comes in sticks as in FIGURE 224. Cut off the same amount from each stick. As you work the two pieces together, the chemical action starts—you will have plenty of time to work with it before it sets up like rock. Use a knife of some sort to pack it in the socket (FIGURE 225) and, after cutting the wire on the eye to ½ inch in length, push the eye into the socket to the proper depth (FIGURE 226). Use the knife to cut around the eye and remove the excess epoxy (FIGURE 227).

FIGURE 219. Marking on the nostrils

134

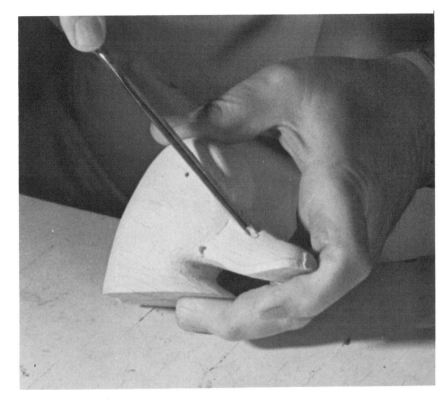

FIGURE 220. Cutting the nostrils with a very fine gouge.

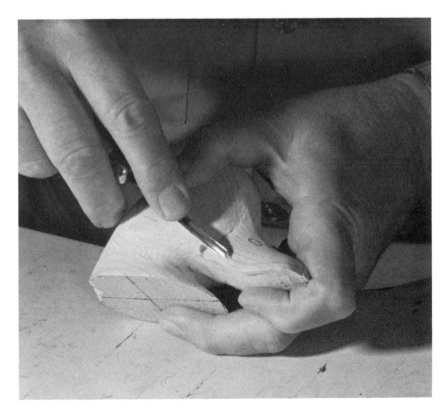

FIGURE 221. Cutting the groove which parallels the bottom of the bill with a very fine V gouge.

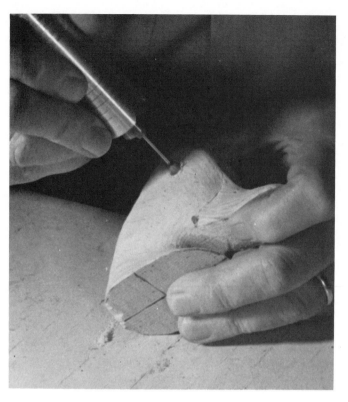

FIGURE 222. Cutting the eye sockets with a small burr.

FIGURE 223. Testing the eye sockets for size.

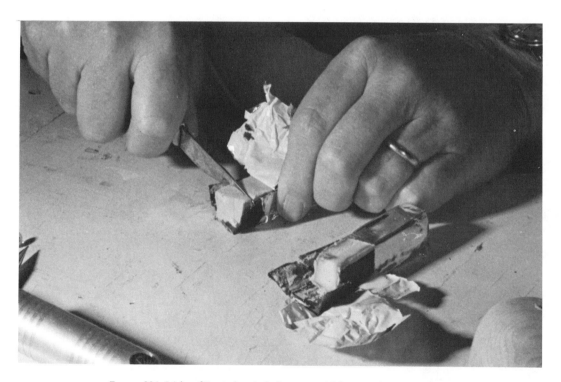

FIGURE 224. Sticks of Epoxybond, the best material for embedding the eyes.

FIGURE 225. Packing the Epoxybond into the eye sockets with a knife.

FIGURE 226. Pushing the eye into the socket to the proper depth.

The process of making decoys can be measured in milestones along the way. I feel we reached our first mark at FIGURES 175 and 176, when the body halves were cut out and fastened together and the head cut and marked. To me, we have reached the seond milestone in FIGURE 228—the body and head carved and sanded and ready for the final steps to becoming a working decoy.

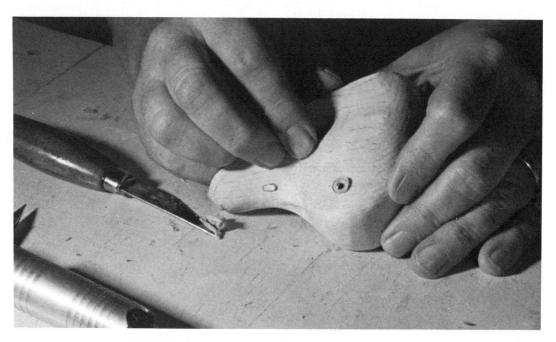

FIGURE 227. The eye, after excess epoxy has been removed with a knife.

FIGURE 228. The body and head carved and sanded.

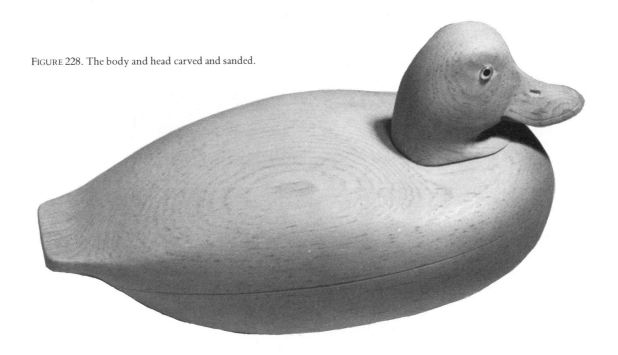

CHAPTER 7

Assembly

THE FIRST STEP TOWARD the final assembly is to unscrew the lag bolts and separate the two body halves. On the upper side of the bottom section we trace the bottom pattern of the decoy itself to give us an idea as to what limits we can use a drill to do the hollowing (FIGURE 229). The hollowing in this case was done with a ¾-inch Forstner bit. This particular bit has no lead spur and so cuts a flat-bottomed hole. The depth guide on the drill press should be set to leave ½ inch for the thickness of the bottom of the decoy. If the wood grain on the drill press table looks a little odd, don't let it worry you. Many years ago, an old craftsman told me that if I were going to work mostly in wood, an 18 × 26 × ¾-inch thick marine plywood extension could be a big help at times. I made one and put it on and have never had any reason to remove it. The hollowing process is shown in FIGURES 230, 231, and 232.

For the sake of the continuity of the illustrations in this section, the body halves were reassembled and the body again mounted on the PoweRarm. Following FIGURE 247 the body was dissembled for the final time and the upper half hollowed in the same way and manner as the lower.

At this point, the plumage pattern is laid out on the body in pencil (FIGURE 233). The base of the sleeper head and the point where you want the bill to lie on the back are also drawn on, because it is obvious in FIGURE 234 that the sleeper head is not going to fit without further modifications. FIGURE 235 illustrates how multiple thin cuts are made on the left-hand underside of the bill until the base of the head and the bill fit down snugly, as in FIGURE 236.

FIGURE 229. Tracing the bottom pattern of the decoy on the upper side of the bottom section.

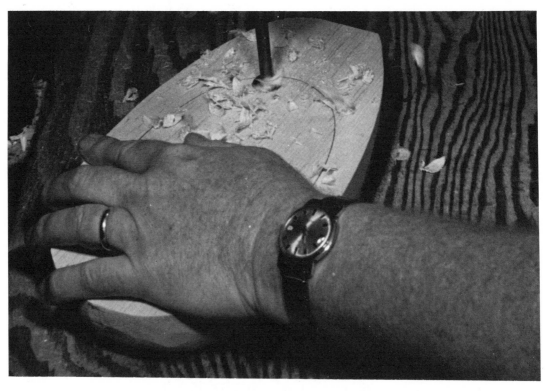

FIGURES 230, 231, 232. The hollowing process.

140

FIG. 231

FIG. 232.

141

FIGURE 233. The plumage pattern laid out in pencil.

FIGURE 234. The base of the sleeper head and the point where the bill will lie on the back drawn in.

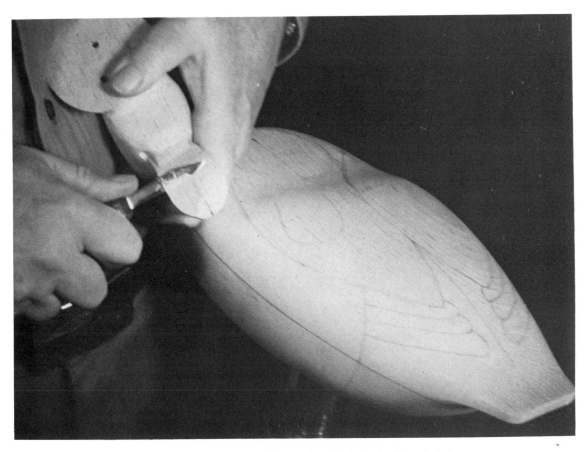

FIGURE 235. Multiple thin cuts being made on the left underside of the bill.

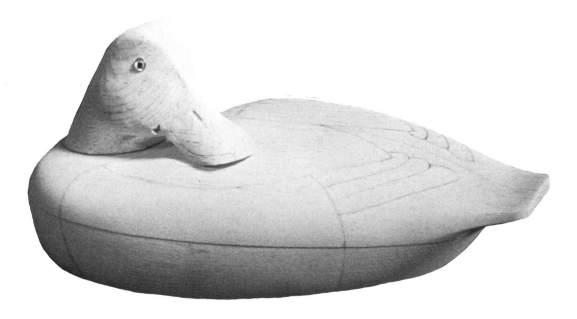

FIGURE 236. The base of the head and the bill fitted down snugly.

143

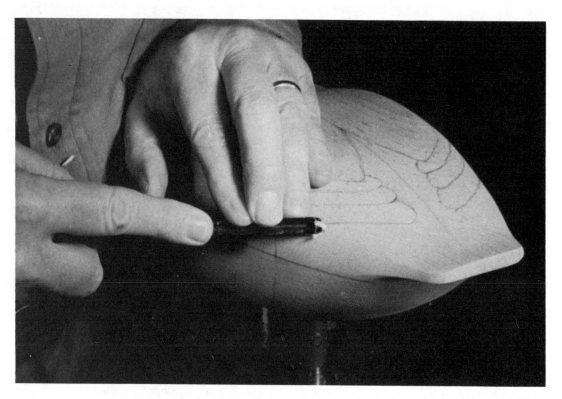

FIGURE 237. Starting at the base of the feather and working out toward the tip with a right-angle parting tool to outline the feather.

Whether or not feathering is put on a working decoy is purely a matter of personal taste. Some carvers, like Elmer Crowell, were apt to put on some primary feathering as a sort of trademark to indicate their better grade decoys. If you want to do the primaries on your own bird, here is how to go about it. Start at the base of the feather and work out toward the tip, using a right-angle parting tool held not quite upright (FIGURE 237). This cut outlines the feather, but makes too much of an actual groove with not enough flatness to the feather itself. By careful use of a very sharp fish tail chisel, the feather can be flattened from the groove out (FIGURE 238). The happy part of this is that the final smoothing and sanding of the feathers can be done very easily with the garnet grit fingernail boards sold in any drugstore (FIGURES 239 and 240). FIGURE 241 shows the touch of feathering completed.

Some of the really fine modern carvers take great pride in doing quite extensive feathering on working decoys, especially if they are birds for their own shooting rigs. The American merganser (FIGURES 242, 243, and 244) is marked: "Fifty Yard Marker—made for my own rig in 1975." It is signed Josef "Buckeye Joe" Wooster, Ashley, Ohio.

144

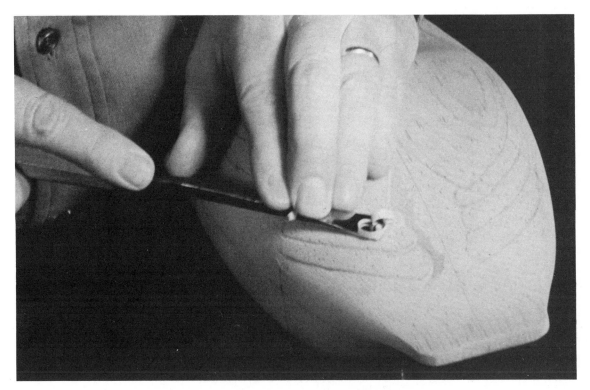

FIGURE 238. Flattening the feather from the groove out with a sharp fish-tail chisel.

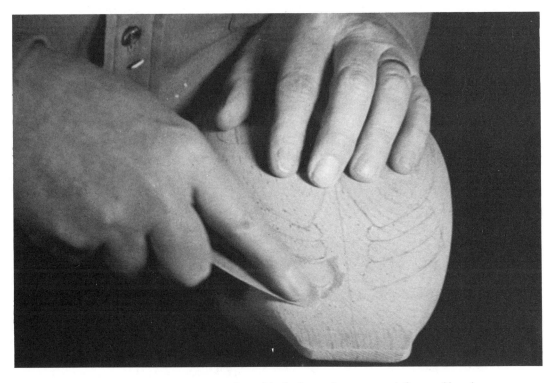

FIGURES 239. Final smoothing and sanding of the feathers, using a garnet grit fingernail board.

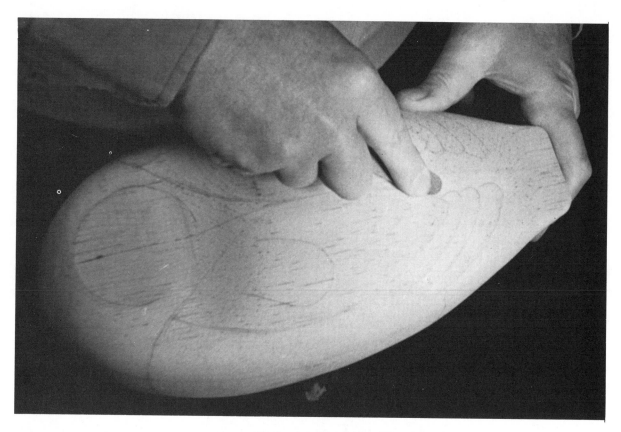

FIGURE 240. Continuation of Figure 239.

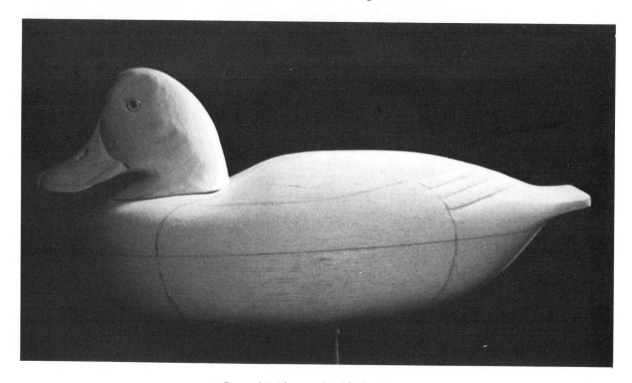

FIGURE 241. The completed feathering.

Fig. 242

Fig. 243

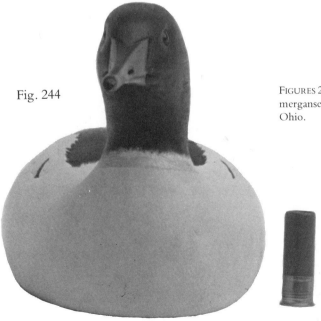

Fig. 244

FIGURES 242, 243, 244. Note the fine feathering on this American merganser made in 1975 by Josef "Buckeye Joe" Wooster of Ashley, Ohio.

Fig. 245

Fig. 246

Fig. 247

FIGURES 245, 246, 247. This whitewing scoter made in 1966 by Al Glasford of Ontario, Canada, is an excellent example of feathering.

Note the fine feathering on the back and tail and especially the fact that no feather sticks up above the body where it could easily be broken. Another outstanding example is the whitewing scoter (FIGURES 245, 246, and 247) made in 1966 by Al Glasford of Ontario, Canada.

As explained above, we now take the bird apart for the last time and hollow the inside of the top half of the body. I have always done on hollow birds what I wish the old makers had done—I carefully sign and date the bird on the inside of the bottom (FIGURE 248).

The earlier hollow birds were a bit of a chore to assemble, since the joints were sealed with white lead paste and then held firmly in place while copper nails were driven in at angles all the way around. These were good joints considering the materials, but they had a tendency to separate after a certain amount of use. We now live in the age of epoxy and, considering its superior bonding power, we would do well to use it. The quick-drying epoxy glues are great for decoys, because it means just that much less drying time before you can pick them up and play with them. As you can see, I use a very high grade palette for mixing the two components of the epoxy (FIGURE 249). Spread the mixture on the surfaces to be joined, being careful to get as little as possible on the outside of the bird (FIGURE 250). Very carefully place the body halves together (FIGURE 251), making sure to get the alignment perfect and to mop up any epoxy that may squeeze out. Great pressure is not necessary—once they seal, you will never get them apart.

FIGURE 248. Signing and dating the hollowed out inside of the bottom.

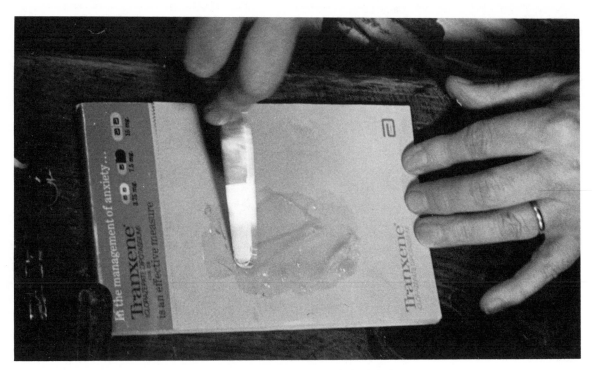

FIGURE 249. Mixing epoxy for joining the body halves.

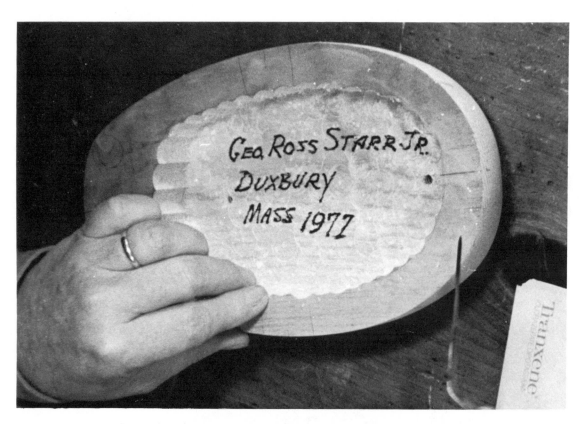

FIGURE 250. The epoxy mixture carefully spread on the surfaces to be joined.

FIGURE 251. The body halves placed together.

A very popular method over the years for securing the head to the body has been to drill a hole up through the body and the head and then fasten them together with a glued dowel. This theoretically strengthens the neck. However, even if you use the driest wood you can find, there is bound to be more shrinkage as time goes by. The big trouble is that the grain of the dowel runs at right angles to the grain in the neck, and when the head and neck shrink, the dowel stays rigid and the neck cracks from front to back. The head doesn't fall apart but it looks messy and, if the dowel is well glued in, it is almost impossible to do anything to remedy the situation.

In the case of a hollow decoy, as we have here, there is good reason to screw the head on from under the upper half of the body. For some reason wood shrinks around screws with much less tendency to split, so it's a pretty sage way to add a bit of strength to the neck, which could very well save it in case of a bad bang. For the few cents extra it may cost, use Everdure screws—neither weather nor salt water will ever bother them. In many areas it was common practice to glue the head on and then put in about four "toe" nails around the base of the head. This works well for the time being, but sooner or later these nails rust and damage occurs around the base of the head. To be perfectly honest, in this case I simply fastened the head on with epoxy (FIGURE 252).

151

As you can see in FIGURE 251, the base line around the head and the body seam don't really form perfect joints and some filling must be done. After trying a number of filling materials of one sort or another, I have finally found what seems to me to be the ideal thing—Duratite surfacing putty. This is a very fine white paste which can be easily handled and forced into the finest cracks. It should be molded around the base of the head and into the line between the body halves (FIGURE 253). The Duratite is a waterproof plastic and has the advantage of being easy to sand. Around the neck base it must be hand sanded, but on the long seams the bow sander works beautifully (FIGURE 254).

FIGURE 252. The head fastened on with epoxy.

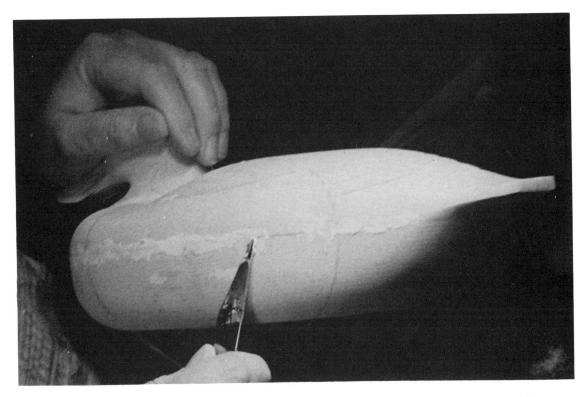

FIGURE 253. Duratite surfacing putty molded around the base of the head and into the line between the body halves.

FIGURE 254. Sanding the long seams with a bow sander.

CHAPTER 8

Painting and Rigging

We have finally arrived at the home stretch in our creation of a working duck decoy. I said earlier that a base or sealer coat is not strictly necessary when using acrylic, but I still like to use one. FIGURES 255 and 256 show the application of a thin, light gray undercoat.

It was not possible to include colored plumage pattern plates in this volume, except for the bluebill we have made from scratch. The very finest plates available were made by Dr. Edgar Burke and may be found in *Duck Shooting Along the Atlantic Tidewater,* published by William Morrow & Company, New York, 1947. However, so many illustrations of decoys are appearing nowadays in sporting and other magazines that it isn't hard to find the colors and patterns. The main consideration is to keep the painting as simple and easy as possible—the decoy will work just as well. However, if you have a feel for painting and want to do a more elaborate job, don't let anyone talk you out of it. A well-painted decoy is a thing of beauty in and of itself.

The feathering on the back of a bluebill is neither white nor black, but grayish white transected by fine wavy black lines. The carvers of Stratford have long duplicated this plumage by using graining combs. These are thin flexible sheets of steel slit at intervals to create what looks like a long-toothed comb. Their true use was to simulate the grain in painted wood—a questionable pastime of the Victorian age. Some years back, Willard Baldwin of Stratford gave me a set which he had

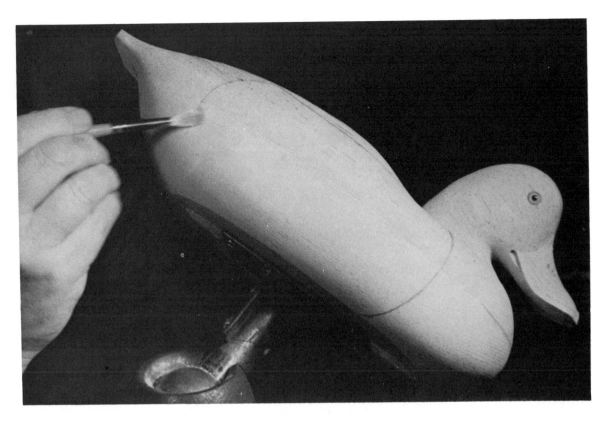

FIGURES 255, 256. Applying a thin, light gray undercoat.

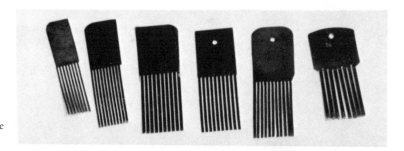

FIGURE 257. A set of graining combs made by Willard Baldwin of Stratford, Conn.

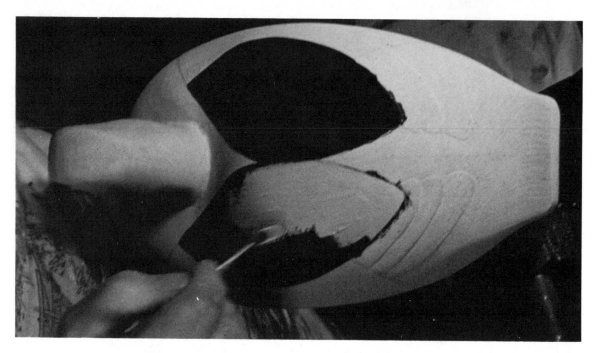

FIGURE 258. A thick coat of light gray is painted over the black areas.

made (FIGURE 257). In FIGURE 258 the back areas have been painted black and allowed to dry and a thick coat of light gray is painted over it. The graining is done as shown in FIGURE 259. I mentioned earlier the quick-drying tendency of acrylics and this can be seen dramatically in FIGURE 260, where the paint dried even before the graining could be completed—and I had even added considerable retarding medium to the gray, which is supposed to slow down the drying. This would not have happened had oil-base paint been used. The rest of the decoy is painted—ending up with the primaries (FIGURE 261). The completed plumage patterns are shown in FIGURES 262 and 263.

When I first started making decoys, I took a leaf from Elmer Crowell's book and made a brand. There is no better way to permanently identify your decoys. The old rule among good gunners that if you find a stray decoy you return it to its owner is a great idea and a good brand can make it easier. One of my cork decoys got loose in Duxbury Marsh one day, floated some eight miles down the bay and around the

156

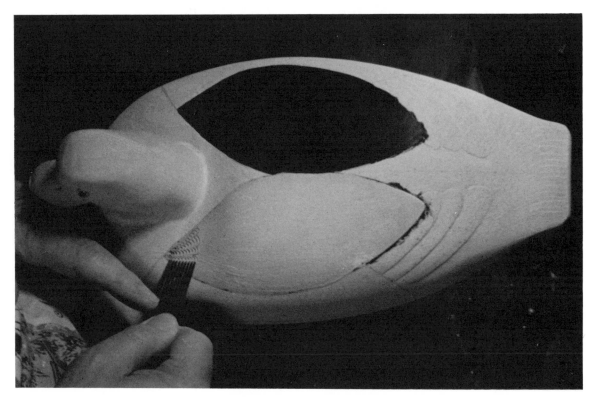

FIGURE 259. Graining with a comb.

FIGURE 260. The quick drying tendency of acrylics can be seen.

FIGURE 261. Painting the primaries.

Gurnet, ten miles up the coast, and was finally found and returned by a man hunting on the North River in Norwell. I carved the pattern from a piece of fine-grain mahogany and did some filling with white enamel so there would be no drag when the sand mold was made. A local foundry cast it for me in bronze and it has served well over the years (FIGURE 264). It is very important to brand before painting. The charred wood acts like a sponge to let water soak into the decoy.

We have a little more work to do before calling the job done. Because we used the PoweRarm as a holder while painting, we are now left with six holes in the bottom which must be filled. Duratite is used as the filler and the excess sanded off (FIGURE 265). If you want a keel, now is the time to put it on. The one shown is ½ × ⅞ inches, with a hole at each end. It should be nailed to the bottom with galvanized box nails (FIGURE 266), the bottom and keel painted (FIGURE 267), and the anchor line and anchor rigged (FIGURE 268). Use only bowline knots—they will never slip and are fairly easy to undo.

Around Stratford and many other areas keels were not considered necessary. A leather loop fastened with a brass screw was used for the anchor line—the leather is easier on the line than any metal (FIGURE 269). They were also prone to use a "tear drop" weight. The tear drop shape is drawn on a piece of board and the drop hollowed to a depth of about ¼ inch at the deepest point. Hot lead is poured into this cavity and allowed to cool. The finished weight is dumped out and a screw hole is

158

FIGURES 262, 263. The completed plumage patterns.

FIGURE 264. The author's bronze brand.

159

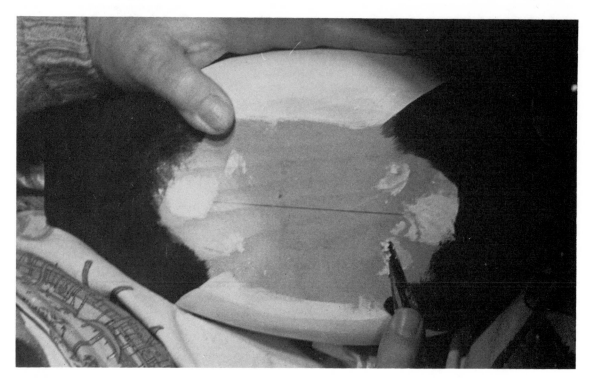

FIGURE 265. Filling the bottom holes made by the PoweRarm, which was used as a holder while painting, with Duratite.

FIGURE 266. Nailing the keel to the bottom with galvanized box nails.

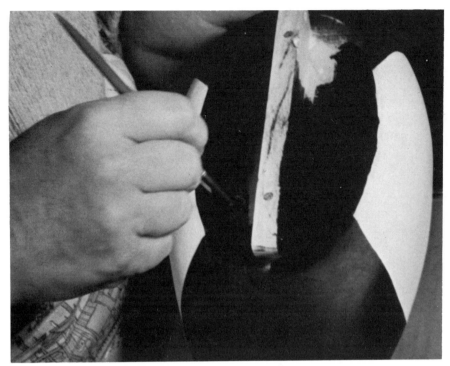

FIGURE 267. The bottom and keel painted.

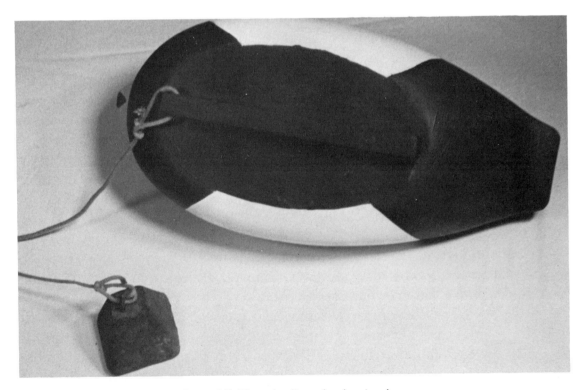

FIGURE 268. The anchor line and anchor rigged.

161

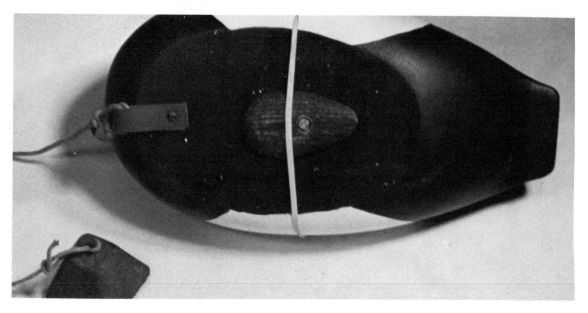

FIGURE 269. A leather loop fastened with a brass screw used for an anchor line.

then drilled. This particular weight was made by Shang Wheeler in days gone by, and you can see by the "grain" on the weight that it was by no means the first to be made in this mold. It is obvious from the location of the screw hole that any rotation will change the side to side distribution of the effective weight. The first step in determining where this weight should be fastened to the bottom is to fill the kitchen sink. A big fat rubber band holds the weight to the bottom in the center line while you wait for the water to come to rest. Set the decoy carefully in the water and see whether it is in trim fore and aft. If the front end is down, carefully reach under and slide the weight back a bit. Keep doing this until the trim is perfect. If the decoy lists to port, again reach under, and without moving it fore or aft rotate the weight a little to starboard. Repeat until there is no list. Now carefully lift the whole decoy out—holding the weight—and mark where the screw should go into the bottom. Fasten the screw and again check for perfect balance. Note that this type of weight is almost impossible to be snagged by any line nor are there any square edges to injure any decoy you may put it next to in a boat. You are now ready to use the rubber band to balance your next decoy.

We have finally arrived at that third stage in this journey where we finally see the product of our labors completed, afloat in its natural element, and ready to go to work (FIGURES 270 and 271). We may not yet be master makers, but we can be proud of what we have created and we are well launched on our way to even greater accomplishments.

FIGURES 270, 271. The completed decoy afloat and ready to do its job.

INDEX